PRAISE FOR
IT'S LONELY AT THE TOP

"Whether you are a CEO, president, or C-suite executive, *It's Lonely at the Top* provides practical advice for anyone wanting to be an inspired leader."

—Jay-Ann Gilfoy

President and CEO, Meridian Credit Union, Toronto Member

"*It's Lonely at the Top* provides a modern-day road map CEOs must follow to inspire themselves and their top teams to be unstoppable during challenging times."

—Bill Tucker

CEO, Omicron Canada, Vancouver Member

"*It's Lonely at the Top* challenges assumptions from CEOs about leadership, showing them how to become inspired leaders focused on impact, not ego, and have a lot more fun along the way."

—Sue Gilpin

CEO, Motion Canada, Toronto Member

"For over a decade, Nancy MacKay has been my CEO peer group forum chair. Applying the leadership strategies in *It's Lonely at the Top* has enabled me to inspire myself and my top team."

—Mike Trotman

CEO, Trotman Auto Group, Vancouver Member

"Nancy distills decades of wisdom into a practical guide for thriving as a CEO and showing up as the best version of ourselves."

—Derek W. Dobson

CEO and Plan Manager, CAAT Pension Plan, Toronto Member

IT'S LONELY AT THE TOP

IT'S LONELY AT THE TOP

CEO STRATEGIES

for Inspiring Yourself and Your Team

Nancy **MacKay**

Forbes | Books

Published by Forbes Books, Charleston, South Carolina.
An imprint of Advantage Media Group.

Printed in the United States of America.

10 9 8 7 6 5 4 3 2 1

ISBN: 979-8-88750-763-7 (Hardcover)
ISBN: 979-8-88750-764-4 (eBook)

Library of Congress Control Number: 2025925666

Cover design by Matthew Morse.
Layout design by Megan Elger.

02-04-2026 2:50

I dedicate this book to the three most inspiring people in my life: Rob, Devon, and Garrett MacKay. Thank you for our twenty-six-plus years of fun family experiences and for joining me on the inspired leadership journey. I love you guys!

CONTENTS

CHAPTER 1
YOU GO FIRST

You find peace not by rearranging the circumstances of your life, but by realizing who you are at the deepest level.
—ECKHART TOLLE

Twenty years ago, I sat across from a brilliant and charismatic CEO who had everything—except happiness. He was privately struggling with feeling overwhelmed, isolated, and burned-out. In that moment, I realized something profound: The tools and strategies that had brought leaders like him to the top were no longer enough to keep them there—or even to help them thrive once they arrived.

One of my clients invited me to be a speaker at his confidential, fourteen-person CEO peer group meeting in Vancouver, and that's what led me to start MacKay CEO Forums. After I did my presentation, I was invited to throw my name in the hat to become its forum chair. About a month later, I chaired my first CEO peer group meeting, and I realized that it doesn't have to be lonely at the top if you surround yourself with successful peers.

That realization led me to create MacKay CEO Forums, and over the past two decades, I've had the privilege of working with more than five thousand CEOs, executives, and business owners across Canada and around the world. Through this work, I've observed the unique pressures CEOs navigate in our rapidly evolving business environment. Whether it's AI and exponential technologies, an evolving geopolitical crisis, or one of a thousand other challenges related to their organizations and their people, CEOs must make hard decisions under great pressure. Along the way, working with these incredible people, I've also discovered something remarkable: The CEOs who truly excel, who *find* deep fulfillment while delivering exceptional results, all share one critical trait—*they've mastered the ability to inspire themselves first before attempting to inspire others.*

This simple yet powerful principle—You Go First—lies at the heart of everything I'll share with you in this book. The truth is, leadership can be lonely. The weight of responsibility, the constant pressure to perform, the challenge of balancing business demands with personal well-being—these are burdens that every leader understands intimately. But it doesn't have to be this way. I've seen time and again that when CEOs commit to mastering the essential elements of inspired leadership, everything changes. Their organizations thrive. Their relationships deepen. Their impact multiplies.

The world of leadership can feel incredibly isolating. A study in *The Leadership Quarterly*, in fact, notes that leadership loneliness is unique and differs from general loneliness.[1] I have spent the last two decades working intimately with thousands of CEOs, executives, and business owners through MacKay CEO Forums, and one of the most

1 Hodar Lam et al., "Leader and Leadership Loneliness: A Review-Based Critique and a Path to Future Research," *Leadership Quarterly* 35, no. 3 (2024): https://doi.org/10.1016/j.leaqua.2024.101780.

consistent messages I hear, regardless of industry or company size, is this: "It's lonely at the top." It's a sentiment that resonates deeply, a quiet acknowledgment of the unique pressures and responsibilities that come with leading an organization. Being surrounded by successful peers not only solves the loneliness challenges but also contributes to the well-being of CEOs, executives, and business owners. According to a Deloitte study, 70 percent of C-suite executives have seriously considered quitting their job for one that better supports their well-being.[2]

When I first conceived of MacKay CEO Forums twenty years ago, it was precisely this sense of isolation that I wanted to address. I saw firsthand that these incredible individuals, the ones making the big decisions and steering the ship, often lacked a true peer group—a confidential space where they could openly discuss their toughest challenges and explore their biggest opportunities without judgment. I believed, and still do, that bringing these CEOs together in carefully curated peer learning groups is transformative, saving them valuable time and leading to far greater success, not just in their businesses but in every aspect of their lives.

Our twenty-year anniversary is a powerful reminder of the impact this simple idea has had. What started with me facilitating a single CEO peer group has demonstrated how CEO forums can address isolation. For us, it has been an incredible journey, one that has profoundly shaped my own understanding of leadership and what it truly takes to thrive in today's rapidly evolving world.

And that brings me to why I've written this book. It was born out of a deep desire to extend the leadership principles and practices

---

2 Jen Fisher and Paul H. Silverglate, "The C-Suite's Role in Well-Being," *Deloitte*, June 22, 2022, https://www2.deloitte.com/us/en/insights/topics/leadership/employee-wellness-in-the-corporate-workplace.html.

we've cultivated at MacKay CEO Forums to a wider audience. While the power of peer support is undeniable, I also recognized a fundamental truth that underpins all successful leadership: Inspiration begins within. You cannot effectively inspire others if you yourself are running on empty.

My aha moment, as it were, came during the height of the COVID-19 pandemic. Overnight, we had to pivot from in-person peer learning groups and events to virtual ones. Amidst the global uncertainty, I was inundated with calls from CEOs worldwide seeking guidance and peer support. Using Zoom as a virtual platform, we were able to offer confidential peer support to CEOs in Canada, the UK, Australia, and the US. Even with virtual peer support, social isolation made leadership very challenging, especially during COVID-19. CEOs couldn't go to the office and meet people in person. All interactions were through Zoom. If loneliness at the top had been an issue before, COVID-19 took it to a whole new level.

As we connected on Zoom for our virtual peer learning group meetings, I consistently found myself asking CEOs, "What about you?" They were so focused on inspiring and supporting the well-being of their top teams, their employees, their customers, their partners—and rightly so—but their own self-care often took a backseat. The blank stares I received in response were a stark reminder of a pervasive detrimental leadership mindset: the need to prioritize everyone else before oneself.

It was in those moments that a profound insight crystallized: True leadership is fundamentally about self-leadership. It's about figuring out how to inspire *yourself* every single day. It's about taking care of your own health because that directly impacts leadership sustainability and performance. Nurturing your personal and family relationships, and dialing up mental toughness and emotional mastery, is also essential because when you do that, you have more energy, more love, and more capacity to give to the rest of the world. And when CEOs are exemplars of self-leadership and they learn how to inspire themselves to be the best version of themselves every day, they are able to inspire their top teams to learn the self-leadership tools in this book so they, in turn, can inspire all employees and create a culture of self-leadership.

True leadership is fundamentally about self-leadership. It's about figuring out how to inspire *yourself* every single day.

This book, *It's Lonely at the Top: CEO Strategies for Inspiring Yourself and Your Team*, is my practical tool kit for inspired leadership. I used the unusual time during the pandemic to dig deep, lock myself in my office, and create a framework for CEOs and their top teams, as well as those who aspire to one day reach the C-suite. My family—including my husband and twenty-something-year-old kids—were my guinea pigs, and then I began to share it more widely, starting with the CEO group that I've been chairing for sixteen years. The feedback I got from my CEO group was that it was the best CEO retreat we had ever done (even though it was a two-day Zoom retreat). This gave me the courage to train all of our forum chairs around the world so they could benefit and also deliver the "Inspired Leadership—You Go First" two-day CEO retreat with all of our one hundred-plus peer learning groups around the world. What was astounding was that the principles resonated so much; they were applicable to everyone, from university students to C-suite leaders. This is not another collection of abstract leadership theories. Instead, it's a distillation of two decades of working with inspiring leaders, coupled with my own personal journey of growth and discovery. My intention is to share the core self-leadership principles and actionable strategies that have proven to be transformative, starting with the most crucial element: you as the CEO of your company and an exemplar for your top team.

But this book is more than a guide—it's an invitation to join a community of CEOs who are committed to our dream of populating the world with inspiring leaders and making the world better, one day at a time. You'll create your own road map to inspired leadership mastery, supported by the insights and experiences of CEOs who have walked this path before you.

Defining Success: Leading from a Place of Inner Strength

Before we dive into the specifics, let's establish a clear understanding of what inspired leadership truly looks like. In the context of You Go First, success isn't solely measured by bottom-line results or external recognition, although those are often positive byproducts. True success in inspired leadership begins with a deep sense of self-love, purpose, unstoppable confidence, and well-being. And with being an exemplar for your top team and others to inspire them to show up as their best selves.

During that time of COVID-19 when I was writing, I thought deeply about what compelled me to jump out of bed every morning at four o'clock, excited for what the day would hold—the challenges and the wins. I considered what I did to inspire myself so that I could show up as my best self. I realized that the inspiration and energy and strength came from ten core areas. My relationships. My passion. My time. My health. My mastery of ego and emotions. My drive for social contribution and shared experiences. My willingness to take 100 percent responsibility in all areas of my life. This book's ten mastery areas are what we call our MacKay Mastery Model for Inspired Leadership—You Go First!:

- **Time mastery:** how to maximize your individual productivity using a personalized approach so you can be strategic about how you spend your time and whom you spend it with (and so you can make the biggest impact on all areas of your life)
- **Ego mastery:** how to show up as the best version of yourself every day by parking your ego and learning to stop judging yourself, the people around you, and your circumstances
- **Emotional mastery and mental fitness:** how to show up in a positive emotional state 80 percent of the time
- **Proactive health mastery:** how to have a healthy lifespan and make health your number one priority; I've learned from CEOs who didn't make health their number one priority that dead CEOs don't meet their targets
- **Relationship mastery:** how to love every human being, including yourself (but not necessarily all of their/your behaviors)
- **Passion mastery:** how to jump out of bed every morning feeling like you just can't wait to get started on making the biggest contribution in all areas of your life
- **Innovation mastery:** how to come up with new ideas, take action, and fail fast

- **One hundred percent responsibility mastery**: how to be self-led and take ownership of all areas of your life
- **Shared experience mastery:** how to share real stories of mistakes you've made and lessons you've learned instead of telling people what to do
- **Social contribution mastery:** how to make the biggest contribution to causes that are aligned with your passion and purpose

Recognizing the importance of building mastery in those ten areas—not only in business but also personally, within my family and the relationships that matter most—was the genesis of the MacKay Mastery Model. For many years now, we've helped thousands of business leaders by sharing the tools and tactics to become inspired leaders.

Now, it's your turn.

This isn't a plug-and-play solution. You're embarking on a lifelong journey that will help you become the best version of yourself, as a CEO and as a human being. Imagine a CEO who navigates challenges with resilience, makes decisions with clarity, and fosters a positive and inspiring environment around them. This isn't someone who is constantly battling burnout or sacrificing their health and personal life for the sake of the business. Instead, they operate from a place of inner strength and unstoppable confidence, fueled by self-awareness, a clear sense of purpose, and healthy boundaries.

Inspired leadership, therefore, is about the following:

- **Leading by example, starting with yourself.** You cannot expect your team members to prioritize their well-being if you aren't prioritizing your own. (If you are reading this and realizing you rarely consider your own well-being because you are so focused on your people, this book is definitely for you!)

- **Cultivating a mastery mindset.** Inspired leaders recognize that leadership is a lifelong journey of continuous improvement (and a continuous learning mindset), driven by developing daily success habits and practices and celebrating progress and supported by both personal reflection and external feedback.
- **Using a strategic approach to design your life.** True leadership effectiveness requires a strategic approach to setting priorities, where your self-care and family care are your top priorities, enabling long-term career success and fulfilment with few or no regrets.
- **Transforming traditional approaches to leadership.** Inspired leaders move away from outdated command-and-control models or micromanagement toward creating space for their top teams and others to become inspired self-leaders.

Next, we'll explore the critical importance of cultivating a *judgment-free mindset*, the fundamental tool kit for inspired self-leadership.

The Power of Judgment-Free Self-Leadership

Judgment-free self-leadership is a commitment to stop judging yourself, others, and your circumstances. It requires a daily success habit of loving yourself, loving others, and accepting versus resisting your circumstances (throughout the book, I'll share some of the success habits that have helped transform the lives of thousands of

CEOs in our peer groups, and their top teams). For example, in the relationship mastery chapter, we define love as (1) being openhearted and judgment-free, (2) telling the truth, and (3) being unconditional (even if you don't love all of the behaviors of others) with all relationships, including how you treat yourself every day.

One of the most significant obstacles to both our own inspiration and our effectiveness as leaders is the constant daily thoughts of judgment—both of ourselves and of others. There are eight billion people on the planet, and we all have an ego (a.k.a. judge) that gets in the way of our success and causes a lot of stress and anxiety. Our ego has a very loud inner critic, that relentless "judge," as I call it, often whispering (or shouting!) messages of inadequacy, doubt, and comparison. We judge and beat ourselves up for our mistakes, our bad decisions, our performance, our appearance, our very worth. And this internal judgment inevitably spills over into how we perceive and interact with the world around us, leading us to judge and label other people as wrong, including our teams, our competitors, our spouses, our kids, and even our circumstances.

Judgment-free leadership is the conscious practice of noticing and quieting our inner judge and approaching ourselves, others, and situations with curiosity, compassion, and love rather than condemnation. It's about recognizing that everyone, including ourselves, is on their own journey, doing the best they can with the knowledge and resources they have at that moment. The truth is, we don't always show up as the best version of ourselves, and neither do the people around us. Judgment-free leadership is about treating every person as a human being with love and respect, especially when they are not showing up as their best self.

What does judgment-free leadership look like in action? Here are some key indicators:

- **Self-love:** You treat yourself with the same kindness and empathy you would offer someone you love who is struggling. You acknowledge and learn from your mistakes without beating yourself up. You let go of imposter syndrome and extreme perfectionism. According to researcher Amy Finlay-Jones, author of the *Handbook of Self-Compassion*, "It's not about letting ourselves off the hook" but about balancing kindness to self with learning and growth.[3] You take time on a daily basis to accept and learn from your mistakes and to celebrate big and small wins as an intentional strategy to quiet your judge, park your ego, and inspire yourself.
- **Empathy:** You strive to understand the perspectives and experiences of others, even when you don't agree with them. You listen to understand, rather than listening to respond or find fault. You listen first, listen 80 percent of the time, quiet your judge, and step into others' shoes before you interact with them.
- **Curiosity:** When faced with challenges or unexpected behavior, and when getting frustrated, you notice and quiet your judge before you interact with another person. Your first instinct is to ask questions and seek understanding, rather than letting your judge jump to conclusions or assigning blame.
- **Focus on learning and growth:** You accept that you are far from being perfect and that you have the rest of your life to learn and grow and show up as your best self. Mistakes are viewed as opportunities for learning and improvement, both for yourself and your top team. The focus shifts from "Who

3 Amy Finlay-Jones, Karen Bluth, and Kristin Neff, eds., *Handbook of Self-Compassion, Mindfulness in Behavioral Health* (Cham, Switzerland: Springer, 2023).

is to blame?" to "What can we learn from this?" (And then to "How do we apply those lessons?")

- **Focus on what you can control:** You accept that people and situations are often imperfect, and you focus your energy on what you can influence rather than dwelling on what you cannot. When you notice yourself blaming others and/or your circumstances and having a victim mindset, you quiet the judge and ask yourself, "What can I do to accept my reality and move things forward in a positive direction?" You say to yourself and others, "I choose to accept my reality, and I'm ready to come up with a plan to move forward in a positive direction." A lot of stress, anxiety, and suffering is caused by our judge wanting us to resist versus accept our reality.
- **Judgment-free communication:** You create a safe, judgment-free, and trusting environment in which people feel comfortable sharing their ideas, challenges, and even mistakes without fear of judgment or reprisal. We create this safe, judgment-free environment in our CEO peer groups so members can put all of their business, family, and personal issues on the table and know that they have fourteen CEOs and their forum chair who are there to support them. We challenge all of our members to create this safe, judgment-free space when they are working with their top teams so they, too, can put all of their business, family, and personal issues on the table and have their CEOs and top teams there to support them. Our ninety-day planning tool for CEOs includes business, family, and personal goals so they can show up as human beings with their top teams. Our members share their ninety-day plans with their top teams and have their top team members share

> their ninety-day plans with the entire top teams in return. This is a game-changing tool to create a culture of judgment-free, inspired self-leaders who can be very authentic and transparent so they can support each other in all aspects of their lives.

The connection between self-love and inspiring others is profound. When you cultivate a sense of acceptance and compassion toward yourself, it naturally extends outward to how you interact with others. You become more attuned to their needs, more understanding of their struggles, and more capable of fostering their growth. As Dr. Shauna Shapiro beautifully articulates in her book, *Good Morning, I Love You*, the journey of leadership, like the journey of life, begins with loving and accepting ourselves. She writes:

> We must change our mind-set from one of self-improvement to one of self-liberation. Self-liberation means freedom from our limiting beliefs, our misguided idea that there is something wrong with us that needs to be "fixed." Our constant attempts to "get it right" and to be "perfect" leave us in a state of exhaustion, never resting in the present moment, never happy with who we are.[4]

Daily Success Habits: Cultivating a Judgment-Free Mindset

Building a judgment-free mindset is not a one-time event; it's an ongoing practice, a daily discipline. Here are three key habits you can begin incorporating into your daily routine today (yes, right now!).

---

4 Shauna Shapiro, *Good Morning, I Love You: Mindfulness and Self-Compassion Practices to Rewire Your Brain for Calm, Clarity, and Joy* (Sounds True, 2022).

HABIT #1: POSITIVE SELF-TALK MANTRA

Pay attention to your judge and negative inner dialogue. When you catch yourself engaging in negative self-talk or judgment, start by celebrating that you caught your judge. I learned this very powerful success habit to help quiet my judge from Shirzad Chamine, author of *Positive Intelligence*. I also learned, from one of my coaches, how to replace my judge with a daily positive self-talk mantra. Here is an example of my daily mantra, which I've coached hundreds of CEOs to use several times a day, in particular during challenging times:

- I am enough.
- I am a gem.
- I am a beautiful person.
- I am a lovable person.

Repeat your mantra to yourself several times throughout the day, especially when you notice the judge creeping in. This simple practice can begin to rewire your internal narrative immediately.

HABIT #2: A MORNING POSITIVE INTELLIGENCE ROUTINE

I dedicate the first twelve minutes each morning to a positive intelligence mental fitness practice that helps me be still, center myself, and access my positive inspired brain (I recently completed the eight-week positive intelligence program developed by Shirzad Chamine). This morning practice sets a positive tone for the day and makes it easier to navigate challenges from a place of calm and clarity. This daily success habit has dramatically reduced my stress and anxiety and improved my performance and relationships with the people around me. This positive intelligence morning practice has replaced my meditation practice, requiring less time and providing higher impact. Throughout the day, I also use a few minutes of quiet breathing (I use the 4-7-8 breathing technique, which you can easily read up on) when I'm getting ready for a difficult conversation or challenging meeting.

Science firmly backs the power of positive intelligence, as Shirzad's organization makes clear:

> Your brain is made up of neurons. When a signal travels down a neuron, it results in activation of other neurons based on synapses that connect neurons. But there are multiple choices for which direction the signal would travel. The question is which neuron will be activated. Every time a neuron activates another neuron, they become more closely wired together, making it more likely that the signal will go in that direction the next time around. This constitutes a "neural pathway."
>
> This is how a repeated action becomes an automatic habit. In Positive Intelligence, we use the powerful 10-second PQ Rep technique as a way of intercepting the old Saboteur responses, so we can pause and choose a new Sage response. Repetition results in Sage neural pathways (muscles) to counter the old Saboteur muscles. That is why our training results in sustained change, as opposed to results fading over time. Mental fitness is about building mental muscles and not just stopping at insights.[5]

5 "The Science of Positive Intelligence," *Positive Intelligence*, accessed June 12, 2025, https://www.positiveintelligence.com/science/.

HABIT #3: AN EVENING GRATITUDE PRACTICE

Before going to bed each night, take a few moments to reflect on your day with gratitude. If you capture your thoughts in a gratitude journal by your bedside table, you might even enjoy better sleep each night because your brain will be filled with positive thoughts. You can write a few bullet point notes about whom and what you are grateful for. They could be big or small things—date night with your spouse/partner, recovering from a sports injury, a successful meeting, a beautiful sunset, getting a promotion, a fun meal with family. Writing down even one or two things you appreciate shifts your focus from what might have gone wrong to what went right. Gratitude is the antithesis of stress and anxiety. This evening practice helps you end the day on a positive note and reinforces a mindset of appreciation rather than judgment.

The best thing about this habit is that gratitude will become second nature to you throughout each day. This reframes how you face difficulties and challenges and helps set the tone for inspired leadership.

CEO Success Story

I've had the privilege of witnessing countless transformations in the CEOs I've worked with. One story that particularly illustrates the power of moving from a self-critical mindset to inspired self-love involves a stressed-out CEO who was about to quit.

Mark was a brilliant and driven CEO. His company had just experienced its best year ever, and by all external measures, he was a resounding success. He'd been written up on the cover of a business journal. He was a "CEO to watch." Yet, at the start of one of our coaching sessions, he confessed he was completely burned-out and considering *quitting*. "I'm exhausted," he admitted. "I think I want to find something else to do with my life."

I was taken aback. From the outside, he looked like he had it all together. (Though I have learned that how things look from the outside is often not the truth—which is why the confidential nature of our peer groups is so important.)

"What's going on?" I asked.

He explained that despite the record-breaking year, he felt an intense pressure, driven by his own internal expectations and perceived industry demands, to "10x the business." He had set these massive new goals and was pushing himself relentlessly to achieve them, to the detriment of his health and personal life.

"Who is telling you that you *have* to 10x the business?" I inquired. "Is it an investor? The board?"

He paused. "No, it's just me," he finally said. "It's just … what we should be doing right now."

But was it?

That's when it became clear: Mark's relentless drive was fueled by a deeply ingrained sense of never being good enough. His inner judge was constantly pushing him, telling him he needed to work harder, achieve more, and sacrifice everything in the process. He admitted to not taking a vacation all year, neglecting his stay-at-home wife and kids throughout the summer, and ignoring concerning health symptoms. His doctor had given him a stark warning about his weight, his stress levels, and his two-scotch-a-night habit.

We began working on helping Mark become aware of his inner judge and the damaging narrative it was perpetuating. We explored the concept of the ego wanting us to suffer, constantly comparing ourselves to others and feeling inadequate (which is why ego mastery is one of the ten areas of mastery in our model). He realized that the harsh judgment he directed at himself was also coloring how he interacted with his team, creating unnecessary pressure and tension. He was also judging his circumstances, feeling compelled to chase unrealistic growth targets based on perceived market conditions rather than his own values and well-being.

We focused on developing strategies to help Mark "park his ego," as I like to say—to become aware of the judgmental thoughts and choose a more compassionate and empowering response. Our ego is our judge. We worked on shifting his mindset from one of constant striving and self-criticism to one of self-acceptance with a focus on sustainable success. We also implemented practical tools such as my ninety-day planning framework to help him regain control of his time and prioritize his health and relationships alongside his business goals.

The transformation was remarkable. We started with Mark focusing on self-love and using a powerful daily mantra ("I'm enough, I'm a gem, I'm a beautiful person, I'm a lovable person"), and it was a game changer for his self-confidence to set boundaries and free up time for his health and family. He also prepared an inspiring, rather than overwhelming, ninety-day plan, and we identified game changers (people with a proven road map to success and willingness to share it) who could help him with each goal to save him time and give him more courage and confidence to achieve success without burnout.

As Mark quieted his inner critic and began to accept himself, he became a more present and effective CEO. He started taking care of his health, spending quality time with his family, and even took a much-needed and long-overdue vacation. His perspective on business growth shifted from a relentless pursuit to a more intentional and sustainable approach. Today, Mark is still leading his very successful company as a leader and disruptor in his industry, thriving both professionally and personally. His story is a powerful testament to the fact that true leadership stems not from constant self-criticism but from a foundation of self-love and unstoppable strength.

Build Your Mastery: Shifting from Criticism to Your Best Self

Developing a judgment-free approach requires conscious effort and the adoption of specific tools and strategies. One powerful framework we use at MacKay CEO Forums to foster more effective and less judgmental communication is the CVA Communication Framework: Caring, Vulnerable, Assertive.

Showing up as the best version of yourself every day is about showing up as a caring, vulnerable, and assertive human being every day. Your judgment-free, authentic self is capable of loving yourself and every human being (even if you don't love their behaviors).

This framework provides a structured way to communicate your needs and feelings while respecting the other person's perspective, effectively parking the ego, as we discussed. It involves showing up in your interactions as a caring, vulnerable, and assertive human being.

I can recall one CEO who was in conflict with his board chair, who was the former CEO and founder of the business.

The CEO kept fighting with the board and calling the board chair a micromanager and told him to stop talking to his top team because he was causing all sorts of chaos and confusion as to who was in charge and able to make decisions. The CEO also blamed the board chair for the poor results of the past quarter. He told the board chair that he was going to quit if the chair didn't stop causing so many problems.

It was a dysfunctional and unproductive situation.

This CEO called to ask my advice, and I let him know that he would likely get fired if he didn't learn how to show up as a CVA—something we will refer to over and over.

Caring: The better way to communicate in this situation was to say: "As the board chair and founder, you are really important to me, and I want to have a great long-term relationship with you. I want to collaborate with you and do everything I can to ensure the success of this business going forward."

Vulnerable: "I want to apologize for not treating you with respect and fighting with you during our previous meetings. I'm not proud of myself, and I certainly have not been showing up as the best version of myself. I'm going to work on improving my ability to have open and honest conversations with you when I get frustrated. I want you to know that I'm very concerned about my top team, as they get very confused when I make a decision and then you override my decision."

Assertive: "My request is that we meet on a weekly basis for thirty minutes so we can discuss any major decisions that I plan to make to ensure you are comfortable with those decisions. This way, we can avoid confusing my top team. And we can work more closely together to collaborate on accelerating the performance of the business. How does that sound to you?"

These elements are so important. By being caring, leaders can begin by expressing that the relationship and the other person matter to them. This creates a foundation of connection and trust. A caring statement can be as simple as, "You really matter to me." My overarching goal is to show up with a caring, openhearted, and loving approach in every interaction. I may not love someone's behavior in the moment, but I still care about them as a human being.

Vulnerability means you share how you are feeling in the situation, without playing the blame game. This allows you to express your feelings, needs, and concerns authentically. Here's a simple example: You have a packed schedule, and you have agreed to a fifteen-minute meeting to start at three. The person hops on Zoom six minutes late. Using our CVA framework, you could start with a caring "I'm grateful for our time together today." Then, you could vulnerably state, "I am disappointed that we are starting our meeting late, as I don't think we'll have enough time to make a decision today."

The assertive piece means you address what you need or what you would like to see happen moving forward. This ensures that your needs are addressed respectfully. Continuing the example, you might add, "Going forward, if you anticipate being late, I would appreciate a heads-up. And could we find a time first thing tomorrow morning to make a decision?" Coming full circle to caring and handling it this way ensures no resentments and that the relationship can move forward in a healthy way.

The CVA framework helps to de-escalate potential conflict and maintain positive relationships by focusing on clear, respectful communication rather than judgment and blame. It allows you to address issues directly while preserving trust and fostering a more collaborative relationship.

To self-assess your current judgment patterns, start by paying attention to your thoughts and reactions in different situations. Ask yourself the following:

- Am I quick to find fault in myself or others? (We are often our own worst critic.)
- Do I often jump to conclusions without seeking all the information?
- Do I tend to label people or situations as good or bad, right or wrong?

- How do I typically respond when someone on my team or in my personal life makes a mistake?
- How do I talk to myself when I make a mistake?

Keeping a journal for a few days can be a helpful way to identify recurring judgmental thoughts and patterns. Or you can simply observe yourself. Remain mindful of these unhealthy patterns.

To actively shift your mindset from criticism to being your best self, try these tools:

- **Ask open-ended questions:** Instead of making assumptions or accusations, ask questions that invite understanding. For example, instead of thinking, *Why are they always late?* try asking, *What happened that made it difficult to be on time today?*
- **Seek the "gift":** When faced with a challenging situation or someone's perceived mistake, ask yourself, *What's the gift in this?* This prompts you to look for potential learning opportunities or unexpected benefits, shifting your focus away from judgment.
- **Practice taking 100 percent responsibility:** Instead of blaming others or external circumstances, ask yourself, *What is my responsibility in this situation? What could I have done differently?* This empowers you to focus on your own actions and potential for learning and growth.

These techniques can keep you from slipping into the judge mindset.

Deeper Dive: Integrating Mindfulness

As we continue to explore the You Go First principle, integrating mindfulness practices can significantly enhance your ability to cultivate a judgment-free mindset. As defined in *Psychology Today*, "Mindfulness is a state of active, open attention to the present. This state is described as observing one's thoughts and feelings without judging them as good or bad."[6]

Consistent mindfulness can help break the judge's hold on you.

As Shauna Shapiro, one of the world's leading scientists on mindfulness, suggests in *Good Morning, I Love You*, cultivating self-compassion through mindful awareness is a powerful way to soften the inner critic and build a foundation of self-acceptance. This inner shift has a ripple effect, allowing you to lead with greater empathy and understanding and, ultimately, more inspiration.

Identify Your Game Changers

In the journey of inspired leadership, you don't have to go it alone. This is one of my main purposes in writing this book—to make sure every CEO knows this. In fact, actively seeking out game changers in all areas of your life is a crucial element of continuous growth and success. Surrounding yourself with game changers will give you greater courage and confidence to show up as your best self every day. You will be able to park your ego, quiet the judge, and achieve greater success in all areas of your life.

At MacKay CEO Forums, we define a game changer as someone who

- is no better than anyone else,
- has a proven road map to success in a specific area that will help you achieve your goals, and
- is willing to share their knowledge and experience.

---

6 "Mindfulness," *Psychology Today*, accessed April 10, 2025, https://www.psychology-today.com/us/basics/mindfulness.

Game changers are able to help you achieve your business, family, and personal goals. For example, game changers can be board members, top team members, mentors, coaches, advisors, peers, friends and family, parenting coaches, doctors, personal trainers, sports coaches, or even authors and thought leaders. The key is to adopt a mindset of constantly seeking out individuals who have "been there and done that" in areas where you want to grow, whether that's in your business, family, or personal life, and to adopt a mindset of leading with generosity by being a game changer for other people who can benefit from your knowledge and experience.

One great example I will share in this area is that of the founder and CEO of a privately held manufacturing company who wanted to set up an advisory board to help him get the business ready to sell in the next three to five years. I shared my experience of setting up my advisory boards and that I always started by looking for a game changer to be my board chair. I explained that the ideal board chair for me is someone who has successfully scaled similar-type businesses and has experience chairing similar advisory boards. Once I have identified the potential board chair by reaching out to my network, I reach out to set up a coffee time to explore their interest in the position. I explain my vision and the commitment I want from my board chair, and that I am committed to supporting my board chair on their goals (I call this leading with generosity and always wanting to be a game changer for others). I then work with this board chair to identify other game changers for the board to help us scale the business. As a result, every board chair (I'm on my fifth) has been a game changer for MacKay CEO Forums (and me personally), over the past twenty years.

Think about your goals. Whom do you know, or whom can you connect with, who has already achieved what you're striving for? My first board chair knew how to scale my vision, and we were a formidable team. Don't hesitate to reach out and learn from others' experiences.

Peer group members gain access to broader professional networks. One MacKay member story that comes to mind that perfectly demonstrates this is that of a CEO who wanted to expand in Europe and become the dominant player in his industry but didn't have any board members with this type of experience. I connected him with a MacKay member who had expanded into Europe and become the dominant player. They had lunch together, and the CEO with Europe experience agreed to connect him with his contacts and to be available to support him on his European expansion. This is an example of how it doesn't have to be lonely at the top if you surround yourself with game changers who are there to support you and give you greater courage and confidence to achieve big goals.

In today's rapidly changing world, relying solely on your own knowledge and experience can be limiting. Actively seeking out game changers is a powerful antidote to the feeling of being alone at the top.

Creating Accountability Partnerships

Another vital aspect of You Go First leadership is the power of creating accountability partnerships. These are relationships in which you and another individual (or a group of people) mutually agree to support each other in achieving your goals and holding each other accountable for taking action. For members of MacKay CEO Forums, their forum chairs and their peer group members are examples of accountability partners. Each member makes bold commitments at the end of each meeting, and they report back on their commitments when they attend their next peer group meeting. Across five thousand members and over twenty years of MacKay CEO Forums, evidence shows that when members do these three things they are 90 percent more likely to take action on bold commitments: (1) they make the commitment to themselves; (2) they make the commitment to their peer group members and their forum chair; and (3) they report back on their commitments at their next meeting so they can track and celebrate progress.

Accountability partners provide encouragement, support, and a gentle push when needed. They offer a space to share your progress, celebrate your wins both big and small, and work through challenges and obstacles. Knowing that someone else is expecting you to take certain steps can be a powerful motivator. This could involve setting shared goals, regularly checking in with each other, and offering constructive feedback.

I value my accountability partners as I work toward achieving mastery and success. They make going through life much more enjoyable and counter the feeling of loneliness at the top.

To give a concrete example of an accountability partner, I value my personal trainers as game changers and create an accountability structure for my health goals because I know I need to be there on Zoom every Tuesday, Thursday, and Saturday morning to do weight training, and Sunday mornings to do Pilates to prevent squash injuries. In my professional life, my board chair is a business game changer. He has been there and done that by scaling much bigger organizations, and I get access to his smarts on an ongoing basis. I learn from his mistakes, and he challenges me to make difficult decisions, especially when the going gets tough.

Having accountability partnerships makes achieving goals easier and fosters greater confidence and courage in all aspects of life through joint accountability. Whether it's finding a game changer to work on your health goals with, a CEO to discuss business strategies with, or a friend to support your personal development, these accountability partnerships can significantly increase your chances of success and reduce the feeling of navigating challenges in isolation.

Remember, the journey of inspired leadership begins with a single step—the decision to *go first.* By embracing a judgment-free mindset, cultivating positive daily habits, seeking out game changers, and creating supportive accountability partnerships, you are laying a powerful foundation for both your personal and professional success.

I am thrilled to embark on this journey with you. Let's turn the often-lonely experience at the top into one of connection, inspiration, and lasting impact, starting with the most important person: *you.* And your top team will be inspired to join you on your journey of inspired self-leadership.

CHAPTER 2

TIME MASTERY

Time is more valuable than money. You can get more money, but you cannot get more time.

—JIM ROHN

Have you ever said, "I don't have time," to your spouse, your kids, people at work, your doctor, your personal trainers, or your pets?

The biggest challenge facing CEOs today is their I-don't-have-time mindset!

I constantly hear CEOs say, "I don't have time to take care of my health, to spend with my spouse and kids, for friends, for hobbies, or for alone time so I can be the best version of myself."

The truth is, you *do* have time. You have 24/7 (minus the seven to eight hours of sleep recommended by longevity experts) and over one hundred waking hours a week.

CEO time mastery is about maximizing your individual productivity so you can make the biggest contribution to all areas of your life—while not sacrificing your health and important personal and family relationships. It's about being strategic about how you spend your time and whom you spend it with.

In my two decades of working closely with thousands of CEOs, I've observed a pervasive challenge, almost an epidemic, that undermines their health, relationships, and overall well-being. It's that I-don't-have-time mindset that gets in the way of CEOs showing up as the best version of themselves in all areas of their lives. This mindset results in CEOs wanting to quit their jobs to find something else to do with their lives because they get overwhelmed and can't see a path toward being a successful CEO without sacrificing everything else in their lives.

My Journey to Time Mastery

As a CEO coach, for years, I've seen firsthand how lonely it can be at the top. CEOs often feel that the weight of their entire organization rests solely on their shoulders, leading to a mindset of perpetual self-reliance. They feel that they can't talk about their toughest business, family, or personal challenges with their board members, their top teams, their spouses, or their friends, and that they have no choice but to lead very lonely lives for as long as they have the top job. This feeling intensified for me when I founded MacKay CEO Forums twenty years ago. I saw a critical gap—CEOs lacked peers who could help them solve problems, maximize opportunities, and avoid sacrificing their health and important personal and family relationships. I could see that CEOs from all different industries had the same problems to solve and opportunities to pursue, and yet they wasted a lot of time because they didn't have access to real stories of mistakes and successes from other CEOs.

As luck would have it, in 2005, one of my clients invited me to be a speaker at his self-moderated CEO peer group in Vancouver, and shortly after, the group hired me to become their forum chair. This changed my life forever because I realized that as a forum chair, I could help fourteen CEOs from all different industries master their time and achieve greater success through confidential peer support. I could see that it was a transformational experience for CEOs to be vulnerable and speak freely about their challenges and opportunities with a group of peers who were there to help them in all areas of their lives. As a lifelong learner, it was transformational for me, as their forum chair, to stay current and relevant and become a lifeline and enduring trusted advisor for CEOs. I remember saying to my husband/business partner, "Peer support for CEOs is what I'm going to do for the rest of my life!" I felt such a surge of excitement. Twenty years later, I'm still chairing CEO peer groups, and I just recently launched a new national $1 billion-plus peer group for CEOs across Canada.

For the first five years, it was just me, building ten fourteen-person locally based confidential peer learning groups across Canada and coaching over a hundred CEOs. Then, I realized the immense potential to help even more CEOs. I knew I could only support 140 CEOs on my own, but if I built a company, we could impact thousands. That meant a significant shift: I had to step into the role of CEO for my own company, a role I hadn't initially envisioned for myself. And, I needed to find independent coaches, consultants, and trusted advisors with extensive experience working with CEOs who believed in the power of peer support to help CEOs master their time and achieve greater success in all areas of their lives.

During this intense period of becoming an entrepreneur, I distinctly remember a time, right after I quit my job as a professor at Simon Fraser University and convinced my husband to quit his job as a banker to pursue this dream, when I experienced days and weeks of panic attacks. I was traveling extensively, I wasn't getting enough sleep, and I wasn't prioritizing my health, my husband, or my kids, who were just starting grade school. We had a significant mortgage and bills to pay, and I was the only income earner for our family. I was deeply immersed in the very struggles I saw my CEO clients facing. It was a personal aha moment. I realized that I needed to learn how to master my time in order to become a successful entrepreneur and not sacrifice what's most important in life—my health and family. I couldn't truly inspire others unless I first inspired myself. This personal crisis, coupled with witnessing the immense pressures and sacrifices made by the CEOs I coached, crystallized my understanding of time mastery. I thought, *There's got to be a better way.*

I was making the mistake of going 24/7 to get my company to the next level. But I began to reflect deeply on what was getting in the way of CEOs' success and what I could do differently to ensure I didn't make those same mistakes. This led to the development of my *How Great CEOs Achieve Time Mastery* workbook (available on our website) and my best-selling *"I Don't Have Time"* coauthored book (eighty-nine pages of very practical strategies) for how to inspire myself every day by being strategic about how I spend my time and whom I spend it with. It starts with recognizing that it doesn't have to be lonely at the top, and that time mastery is a fundamental CEO leadership skill. I'm committed to being very vulnerable in this book, sharing my own journey and the practical tools I've honed over two decades that have allowed me to lead MacKay CEO Forums while maintaining my health and nurturing my most important relationships. This commitment to self-care is not selfish; it allows me to show up as the best version of myself and have more to give to the world.

Defining Time Mastery: Beyond Time Management

I never use the term *time management.* To me, that's a very old-school mindset. It implies merely tweaking to-do lists and organizing tasks. We live in an exponential, AI-enabled world where things move incredibly fast. True time mastery goes far beyond simple management. My definition of time mastery is about maximizing your personal, individual productivity so that you can make the biggest contribution in all areas of your life. It is about strategic prioritization of *how* you spend your time and *whom* you spend it with, rather than a fictional concept of life balance.

I never use the term *life balance.* To me, a lot of suffering is caused by the concept of life balance and having a perfect wheel of life (see the figure later in the chapter). For example, when I coach CEOs on time mastery, I ask them to rate their satisfaction on key business, family, and personal areas of their lives on a scale of 1 (low) to 10 (high). Most CEOs rate themselves quite low on their time-mastery scores. Then I ask them if they want 10/10 on all areas of their lives, and most of the time I get a resounding yes. I do tell them that life is a bumpy ride, and it's not possible to have a 10/10 in all areas of your life all of the time. Time mastery is about accepting your current situation and setting goals to improve the areas of life that you are not satisfied with one quarter at a time (i.e., using our Unstoppable CEO ninety-day planning tool, which you can access on our website). It's also imperative to surround yourself with game changers to help you save time and achieve all of your business, family, and personal goals.

CEO time mastery requires a deeply personalized approach. What works for me—waking up at four in the morning and going to bed at eight o'clock at night to ensure I am optimizing sleep, working out every day, practicing a twelve-minute mental fitness daily success habit, and blocking time for these things as well as for my adult kids, husband, friends, and other family—may not work for every CEO. I openly share my practices, but I emphasize that each CEO must discover their own strategies that align with their personal circumstances and energy levels. The core idea is simple: *Time allocation is about strategic choices, not availability.* You have twenty-four hours in a day, and if you're getting the recommended seven to eight hours of sleep a night, you have over one hundred hours each week to accomplish what you want. The key is to be strategic and intentional about how you allocate those precious hours.

The Three Biggest Time Mastery Mistakes CEOs Make

After working with thousands of CEOs, I've identified three significant mistakes that consistently derail their time mastery and overall success:

1. **The 24/7 trap:** This is the pervasive belief that the only way for a CEO to be truly successful is to work twenty-four hours a day, seven days a week. CEOs caught in this trap literally sacrifice their sleep, health, and personal lives, believing it's the only path to achievement. They might say, "I'll try to get some sleep in if I can" or "I'll spend some time with my spouse and kids, but I really need to just focus on work because it's the only way I can be successful." This mindset is a recipe for burnout, divorces, and severe health issues. It also leads to feeling constantly lonely at the top, despite being surrounded by teams and boards.

2. **The do-it-yourself syndrome:** Many CEOs operate with the mindset that they are the *only* ones good enough, smart enough, or fast enough to get the job done. Face it, they are where they are because they *are* smart and are leaders. But the mindset causes them to roll up their sleeves and try to do everything themselves, rather than leveraging the talents and expertise of others. This is a massive time-waster and prevents exponential growth, both personally and for the business. They often don't have a mindset of actively seeking game changers to help them achieve their goals.
3. **Making decisions in a negative emotional state:** When CEOs are angry, annoyed, frustrated, stressed out, or freaked out, their egos get incredibly loud and they are prone to making bad decisions. These decisions waste a lot of time, damage crucial relationships (such as with their board members), and significantly increase stress levels. While studies vary, it seems the majority of our thoughts are negative. Not only that, when we are stressed and anxious, the optimal part of our brain for decisions and memory decreases its functionality significantly.[7] If CEOs operate from this place, they will be spreading negativity and undermining their own effectiveness.

These three mistakes create a constant cycle of overwhelm and underperformance in the areas that truly matter in a CEO's life. Breaking free from them requires a fundamental shift in mindset and the adoption of new strategies.

7 "Vital Signs," Brain Health, Brigham and Women's Hospital, Harvard Medical School, accessed September 23, 2025, https://brainhealth.bwh.harvard.edu/vitalsigns.

Key Strategies to Master Your Time

For me, time mastery is built on interconnected strategies that move CEOs from these common pitfalls to a place of greater contribution and fulfillment.

TAKE CONTROL OF YOUR WHEEL OF LIFE

This is a powerful visual tool that helps CEOs assess and prioritize all critical areas of their lives. It typically includes elements such as career, health, family, personal growth, social contribution, and personal and family relationships—as well as things you enjoy for leisure (a.k.a. *fun*—for me, this is a weekly squash game with my twenty-six-year-old son who beats me very badly every week and a weekly Zumba dance class with my twenty-four-year-old daughter who cheers me on when I can't keep up with the instructor). Most CEOs don't stop to think about what truly matters to them. People who are very career-driven may be swept up in achieving without ever pausing to ask themselves if they are spending time on what matters to them and with the most important people in their lives. By visually mapping out these areas, CEOs can identify where they are currently investing their time and energy versus where they *want* to be investing it. They can also assess how satisfied they are with all areas of their lives. This foundational step provides clarity on where strategic adjustments are needed. It allows a CEO to intentionally design their time rather than letting their schedule dictate their life.

When I coach CEOs, once they develop this awareness, we develop an Unstoppable CEO ninety-day plan to address any areas of dissatisfaction, such as with their careers, significant others/family, or health.

The wheel of life and Unstoppable CEO ninety-day plan also help identify your game changers to help save you time and achieve goals in these areas.

STEP 1: COMPLETE YOUR WHEEL OF LIFE

Rate yourself on a scale of 1–10 (10 = high) according to how satisfied you are with each aspect of your wheel of life.

Reflect on your assessment: What choices are you making? What are you saying yes to? What are you saying no to? How can you even out your wheel for a smoother ride?

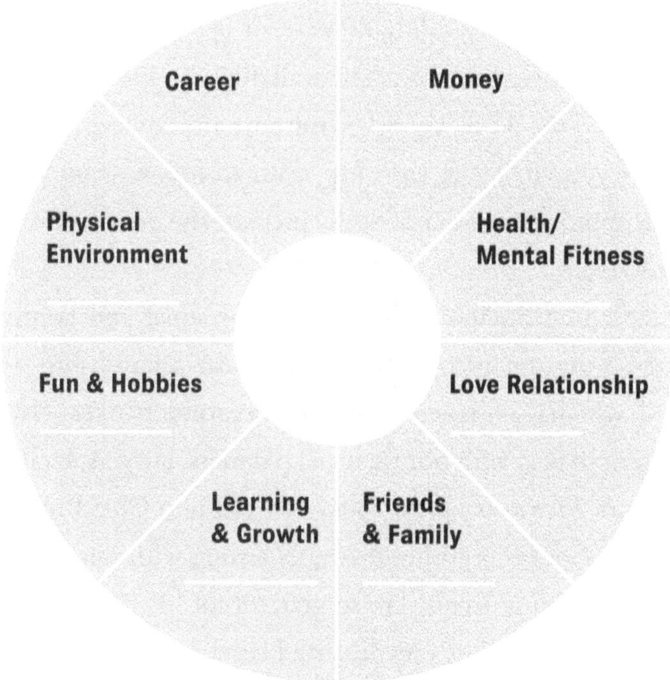

FOCUS ON YOUR STRENGTHS

A core principle of time mastery is to be very intentional about spending most of your time in your areas of strength. This enables you to make your biggest contribution consistently. Many CEOs, driven by the do-it-yourself syndrome, waste valuable time on tasks they are not good at or that drain their energy. The key is to identify your unique strengths, for example, through tools such as StrengthsFinder 2.0 (now CliftonStrengths), and then delegate or outsource activities that fall outside those areas. This isn't about avoiding rolling up your sleeves; it's about optimizing your efforts—and guarding your time. As a CEO, you need to hire for your blind spots, bringing in individuals whose strengths complement your own. This way, you empower your team and free yourself to focus on what you do best, which drives higher performance for everyone involved.

If you strive for spending 80 percent of your time in your areas of strength and delegate or outsource all other decisions and activities, you will avoid the do-it-yourself syndrome and achieve much greater success. If you challenge your top team to follow your 80 percent goal, this approach will dramatically increase the performance of your entire top team.

This same principle holds true for personal and family goals. I realized early on in my twenty-eight-year relationship with my husband, who has a finance MBA and is a former banker, that I could rely on him to deal with our financial planners, lawyers, bankers, and accountants. He's also a great cook—we call him Chef Rob—and he can fix just about everything that goes wrong with our cars, homes, computers, or home gyms. I'm so grateful for his strengths, and I've learned to stay out of his way because I certainly don't have strengths in those areas! This frees up my time so I can spend it with friends and family and maximize my work productivity.

ELIMINATE EGO TALK

Later in this book, there is a whole chapter on ego mastery. However, just as all the mastery areas work together, ego plays a role in time mastery. Our ego is often our biggest time-waster. When a CEO is in a negative emotional state—what I call the "house of ego"—they are prone to reactive decisions, blame games, defensiveness, and trust-busting behaviors. This "ego talk" is also contagious and spreads negativity throughout the organization. For example, a CEO complaining about frustrating interactions with the board or a micromanaging board chair is operating from ego, wasting time and damaging relationships. Conversely, when a CEO operates from the opposite, from the "house of leadership," they never criticize others, they are self-aware, they give credit to others, and they embrace feedback as a gift. Learning to park your ego means recognizing when you're in a negative state, dialing it down, and showing up as your best self. This intentional practice drastically reduces wasted time and stress, improves decision-making, and deepens relationships.

PRACTICE MENTAL FITNESS

This strategy builds directly on mastering your ego, and it also has its own mastery chapter in terms of emotional mastery. When a CEO is "above the line," in a positive emotional state, they are mentally tough and able to access their inspired brain. This state allows for clarity, optimal decision-making, reduced stress, and higher performance. The opposite is being "below the line," in a negative emotional state, in which you're catastrophizing about the future, beating yourself up over the past, listening to your internal judge, and allowing negative thoughts to consume your time and energy. Mental fitness is about the daily discipline of responding instead of reacting to others and to your circumstances. It means intentionally shifting your focus to what you really want, what success looks like, and what your purpose is, rather than getting bogged down by fear, stress, anxiety, and negativity.

USE THE HAPPINESS FORMULA

The happiness formula serves as the fifth critical strategy for time mastery. As CEOs, we waste a lot of time being miserable and playing the blame game when we are not happy with our current situation. By learning to apply the happiness formula to accept or change either your life condition or your expectations when things don't go your way, you can save time and be happy no matter what.

THE HAPPINESS FORMULA

LC = Life Condition

E = Expectation

If LC = E, then ☺

If LC does not = E, then ☹

A huge time-saving strategy is to start by accepting your life condition. We waste a lot of time by not accepting our current reality when we get bad news. For example, how much time do CEOs spend being miserable about getting fired, not getting a promotion, not getting a deal done, not getting a raise, not getting their dream job, etc.

If you can't change your life condition, you can do three things:

1. Accept your life condition.
2. Learn from it to avoid future disappointments.

3. Treat everything in life as a gift. Ask yourself, "How can this current situation be a gift?"

These three steps will get you into a happy state, and you will then be able to save a lot of time and make better decisions going forward. In some circumstances, you can either change your life condition or change your expectations or do both in order to be happy no matter what. *New York Times* best-selling author Richard Carlson outlined five core principles—thought, mood, separate realities, feelings, and the present moment—to help readers cultivate lasting inner peace. His practical approach emphasizes the power of perspective and personal responsibility in achieving happiness.[8] You can learn to reach a happy state even in difficult circumstances.

Embracing this formula consistently contributes to your happiness and saves you a lot of time. This isn't about avoiding challenges but approaching them from a place of knowing you can be happy no matter what when you use the happiness formula on a daily basis.

These five strategies, when adopted intentionally, will help you master your time and achieve greater success in all areas of your life.

Daily Success Habits for Time Mastery

To maximize their individual productivity, CEOs need practical, daily success habits. It's easy to think it's a great idea—but you also need to take action in order to master your time and achieve extraordinary results without sacrificing your health and important personal and family relationships.

---

8 Richard Carlson, *You Can Be Happy No Matter What: Five Principles for Keeping Life in Perspective* (New World, 2006).

HABIT #1: DAILY COMMITMENT TO HEALTH AND WELL-BEING (BLOCK TIME FOR YOURSELF AND YOUR FAMILY)

Self-care and family care are nonnegotiable. For self-care, every single day, CEOs must block time in their calendars for their mental and physical fitness with no excuses. We will talk about this more in the proactive health mastery chapter. The best times for me are first thing in the morning, at four o'clock, and before I go to bed at night at eight o'clock, as these bookend my day in a positive, inspired state. On weekdays, I have thirty minutes to two hours, and on weekends, I have three or more hours each day, but it's blocked in my calendar. I personally integrate my workouts and health appointments into my transparent calendar so my team sees that I walk the talk on health as my number one priority, and I encourage them to have health as their number one priority.

CEO self-care is a personalized approach that needs to be blocked in your calendar seven days a week. It's the only way you can show up as the best version of yourself every day. It's heartbreaking for me to hear so many CEOs say "I don't have time" for annual physicals, colonoscopies, MRI screenings, or physical and mental fitness. I push back on this mindset aggressively. You *do* have time, and you have to make it a priority.

For family care, start by blocking weekly date nights with your spouse/significant other in your calendar. Rob and I would not be celebrating twenty-eight years of being together if we hadn't committed ourselves to weekly date nights, couples counseling and retreats, and vacations (with no kids) as we navigated running a business and raising two kids together. Block date nights with your kids, family dinners, time with friends and family, family vacations, and time for hobbies in your calendar.

Once you've blocked time for self-care and family care in your calendar, your productivity will improve dramatically because your positive brain will understand that you actually aren't available to work 24/7. You'll be a lot more focused on how to spend your time and whom to spend it with when you realize that you need to make the most of the limited time you have available for work activities. You will get much better at setting boundaries and being very intentional about what you say yes to and what you say no to. And, the people around you will see that you are an exemplar of mastering your time so that you can be the best version of yourself every day.

HABIT #2: PRIORITIZE SLEEP

Sleep deprivation is a crisis at the top. Many CEOs believe they can function on four hours or even two to three hours of sleep, leading to mental breakdowns, poor decision-making, and accelerated aging. In an article in *CEO Monthly,* sleep researcher Els van der Horm notes that only 3 percent of us are genetically disposed to function on less than six hours of sleep per night.[9] In other words, it's biologically crucial for CEOs to get the recommended seven to eight hours of sleep per night for longevity and optimal brain health. If a CEO struggles with this, they must seek experts to assess and solve their sleep deprivation challenges. This is a fundamental aspect of taking 100 percent responsibility (another mastery area) for your health and performance.

---

9 CEO Monthly, "CEOs Who Are Sleep Deprived Are Grumpy and Distracted: Here's Why They Need More Sleep," *CEO Monthly*, March 22, 2022, https://www.ceo-review.com/ceos-who-are-sleep-deprived-are-grumpy-and-distracted-heres-why-they-need-more-sleep/.

HABIT #3: DAILY MENTAL FITNESS PRACTICE (MEDITATION/BREATHING)

I recently replaced my traditional meditation practice with an early-morning twelve-minute positive intelligence practice and ten-second positive intelligence repetitions (PQ reps) throughout the day. This is a powerful practice that no one else even needs to know you're doing, and it instantly grounds you and gives you access to your inspired brain. It neutralizes negative emotions, allowing you to be fully present and make better decisions, even in high-stress situations. This is a core tool from the positive intelligence framework, which I highly recommend. But everyone needs to find the mental fitness routine that works for them. Today, there are many mental fitness and meditation apps that can incorporate this into your day. In the context of this chapter, though, the most important thing is to carve out the time—because it is a very effective daily success habit to save you time by giving you greater access to your positive brain throughout the day.

These daily habits build the resilience and clarity necessary for true time mastery. At MacKay CEO Forums, our forum chairs dedicate a full hour with every new member to help them set their time-mastery goals and integrate these practices (more on that in the game changers section).

CEO Success Story

One powerful story that exemplifies the profound impact of time mastery involves a CEO who, despite being incredibly successful in business, found his personal life in complete disarray. This CEO hadn't taken a vacation in years; he literally didn't know how much vacation time he had accrued; and his marriage was crumbling. He was a classic example of someone caught in the 24/7 trap, believing that sacrificing everything for work was the only way to succeed. His kids were strangers—and he never made it to their sporting events or even awards ceremonies.

During a coaching session, I sensed the deep exhaustion and desperation in him. He was at a breaking point, contemplating quitting his job despite his career success because his entire life felt like a wreck outside of work. It was clear he needed an intervention. So, instead of just offering advice, I took a very direct approach, inviting his executive assistant (EA) into the conversation, with his full permission. This was a crucial step, as exceptional EAs are often the game changers of a CEO's ability to master their life.

We began by blocking self-care and family care into his calendar and mapping out his one hundred waking hours per week. We literally blocked time in his calendar for essential nonwork activities: marriage counseling sessions, dedicated time to spend with his kids, and, most powerfully, a two-week family vacation. His EA was there, diligently taking notes, witnessing his commitment to transform his life. We worked through each of the five time-mastery strategies: establishing his wheel of life priorities, identifying areas where he could leverage his strengths and delegate tasks he wasn't passionate about, recognizing how his ego was contributing to his stress, and building mental fitness to approach challenges from an inspired state. We also worked on his Unstoppable CEO ninety-day plan to help him get clarity on his top-three business, family, and personal goals for the quarter and identify game changers to help him achieve his goals with greater confidence and courage.

This CEO was ready to let go of the past and commit to this transformation. The results were almost immediate. After just one coaching session, he booked that two-week vacation with his family (his wife thought he was joking). He began to delegate tasks and shift responsibilities, getting a significant amount of work off his plate. Fast-forward to today, and he is still the CEO of that company, thriving both professionally and personally. This story powerfully illustrates that it's not about finding more time but about making time for what truly matters, and that even the most overwhelmed CEOs can achieve profound transformations when they commit to learning time-mastery strategies and working with their EA as their time-mastery game changer.

It's not about finding more time but about making time for what truly matters.

I also recall another CEO who came to me celebrating her best year ever but admitted she hadn't taken a vacation all year and was questioning if she should quit her job because her personal life was suffering. She couldn't even articulate her personal purpose. Through applying questions such as What does success look like?, What do you want?, and If you knew you couldn't fail, what would you do?, she realized she *did* want to continue as a CEO, but (big caveat) with a great marriage and time for her kids and health. We used the five time-mastery strategies to help her regain control of her life. These are just a couple of examples of how time mastery isn't just a business strategy; it's a life strategy.

Deeper Dive: The Unique MacKay Approach to Time Mastery

As made clear in the foreword of my previous book with Nico Human, called *"I Don't Have Time!" How to Avoid the THREE Biggest Time Mastery Mistakes CEOs Make*, time is the great equalizer. We all have a set amount of it in any day. As I wrote earlier, I don't believe in time management. My approach to time mastery has been developed organically over two decades of intense hands-on experience coaching thousands of CEOs. I believe my insights are unique because I have been in the trenches with CEOs, observing their challenges and pain points and cocreating solutions in real time within the confidential setting of our peer groups.

My work with CEOs is not theoretical; it's deeply practical and rooted in the day-to-day realities of leading complex organizations. "*I Don't Have Time!*" is an eighty-nine-page condensed distillation of this very approach, designed to be highly impactful and immediately actionable for busy CEOs who "don't have time" to read long books.

Identify Your Game Changers: Whom You Spend Your Time with Matters

The concept of game changers is central to all our mastery areas, and time mastery is no exception. However, for time mastery, the game changers you need are not necessarily other time-mastery experts, because I believe this framework is comprehensive. Instead, they are the people who have a proven road map to success to help you achieve your goals and are willing to share it.

This is where I truly think the power of peer groups is essential. At MacKay CEO Forums, we focus on helping CEOs identify and get connected to game changers to help them achieve all of their business, family, and personal goals. For example, one of the first things we offer new members is a one-hour time-mastery goal-setting session with their forum chair. During the coaching session, their forum chair helps them identify potential game changers to help them achieve their goals. Game changers might be on their board or their top team, external advisors, or within our MacKay CEO Forums community of over five thousand Canadian CEOs, executives, and business owners who are current or alumni members.

In addition to the one-to-one coaching, at every full-day fourteen-person confidential peer group meeting, their forum chair facilitates a fifteen-minute Give & Get game changer exchange. Each member has the opportunity to ask for introductions to potential game changers, and their peers help make introductions. For example, one CEO had a goal to become the dominant player in the US and was just getting started. One of his peers had been there and done that before in a previous role, so he offered to meet with him to share his road map to success. Another CEO needed a government relations expert, and he left the meeting with names and contact information of the top-three government relations experts in British Columbia. Another CEO had a personal goal to get a thorough heart assessment because his super-fit CFO had recently died suddenly of a heart attack at the age of fifty-seven. I offered to introduce him to Diamond Fernandez at Heart Fit Clinics, who is saving lives every day across Canada, as I had recently done the AI-enabled heart assessment (and talked my husband into doing it as well).

These peer groups create a confidential environment in which CEOs can speak honestly about their struggles and ask for help. Asking for help and looking for game changers is a sign of strength and will lead to extraordinary time mastery. Whom you spend your time with really matters, and game changers will not only save you time, but they will give you greater courage and confidence to achieve your goals.

My ultimate goal is to equip you to lead with greater courage, confidence, and sustained inspiration, not just for yourself but for your entire top team and, by ripple effect, for everyone you influence.

You can achieve extraordinary results without sacrificing what matters most. Embrace time mastery and surround yourself with game changers, and you will unlock a profoundly more effective and fulfilling leadership journey.

END-OF-CHAPTER CHECK-IN

Rate the following statements on a Likert scale (e.g., 1 = strongly disagree, 5 = strongly agree), and get your score.

TIME MASTERY

- I regularly reflect on how I spend my time across business, family, and personal areas of my life and whom I spend my time with.
- I have a clear, actionable ninety-day plan that I review and revise regularly. And, I have identified a game changer for each business, family, and personal goal.
- I feel aligned in how I prioritize time for health and relationships alongside work.

TIME MASTERY REFLECTION

Where am I spending time out of obligation instead of intention? What would an Unstoppable CEO ninety-day plan look like if I truly prioritized what matters most?

GAME CHANGER PROMPT

Who are my game changers when it comes to time? Who models excellent time mastery? Who can help me refine my priorities and stick to my plan?

CHAPTER 3
EGO MASTERY

The primary cause of unhappiness is never the situation but your thoughts about it.
—ECKHART TOLLE

As human beings, we have an astonishing number of thoughts every day. While we generate thousands of thoughts daily, my experience shows our ego often frames these thoughts negatively. Our ego produces mainly negative thoughts, which can unfortunately lead to a great deal of suffering, including stress, anxiety, mental fitness challenges, poor decision-making, relationship dustups, etc. Shirzad Chamine, author of *Positive Intelligence*, talks about our internal negative voices ("saboteurs") that can prevent us from taking the kind of actions needed to lead us to levels of greater success *and* happiness.[10]

Mastering your ego is not just a psychological concept; it is a critical CEO leadership skill that will improve your well-being, accelerate your performance, and help you achieve relationship mastery, both

10 Shirzad Chamine, "How We Self-Sabotage," Positive Intelligence, https://www.positiveintelligence.com/saboteurs.

in business and in your personal life (and with yourself!). Mastering your ego is so fundamental to CEO success, and when you go first, you will be an exemplar for your top team and you'll inspire them to be on the ego mastery journey with you.

Executive isolation remains a pervasive challenge across industries. I believe that it doesn't have to be lonely at the top, and a key part of that lies in mastering our ego (judge). In the MacKay Mastery Model, I define ego (judge) as the loud voice that emerges when we're in a negative emotional state. As human beings, when we are in a negative emotional state, we judge ourselves, we judge other people, and we judge our circumstances to be bad. The house of ego (see diagram) shows that our ego is all about looking good, being right, getting defensive, playing the blame game, and criticizing others, even ourselves. It constantly tells you that you're not enough, that the people around you are not good enough (your board, top team, external advisors, customers, significant others, kids, etc.), and when you get bad news, you judge your circumstance to be really bad and you catastrophize about the future and beat yourself up about the past.

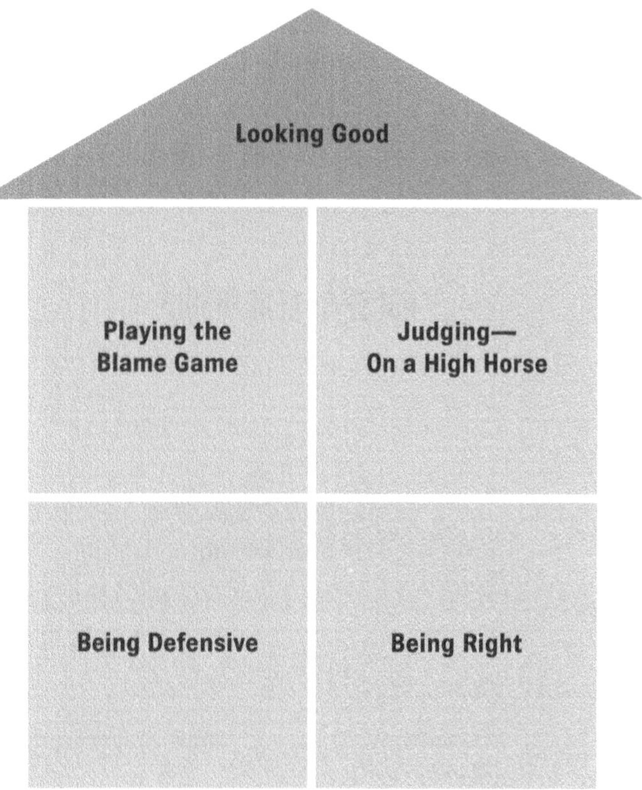

As an inspired CEO, You Go First means you will show up consistently (80 percent of the time, as it's not humanly possible to show up 100 percent of the time) in the House of Inspiring Leadership (see diagram). This is where we park our ego (i.e., quiet our judge), consistently give 100 percent credit to everyone else, and truly believe that feedback is a gift, remaining open to receiving it so we can continuously improve. It means recognizing that you don't have to be the smartest person in the room or look good or have all of the answers.

You let go of being right, getting defensive, playing the blame game, and criticizing others. This shift in mindset is crucial because an unmastered ego frequently gets in the way of a CEO's success. If you're not self-aware, when you are in the house of ego, you will invite others around you to be in the house of ego, and this wastes a lot of time, decreases effective decision-making, and damages relationships along the way. The goal is to have you and your top team show up in the house of leadership 80 percent of the time, and when egos get in the way of success, people apologize, learn from it, and move on.

HOUSE OF LEADERSHIP

SET THE INTENTION OF 80% POSITIVE STATE

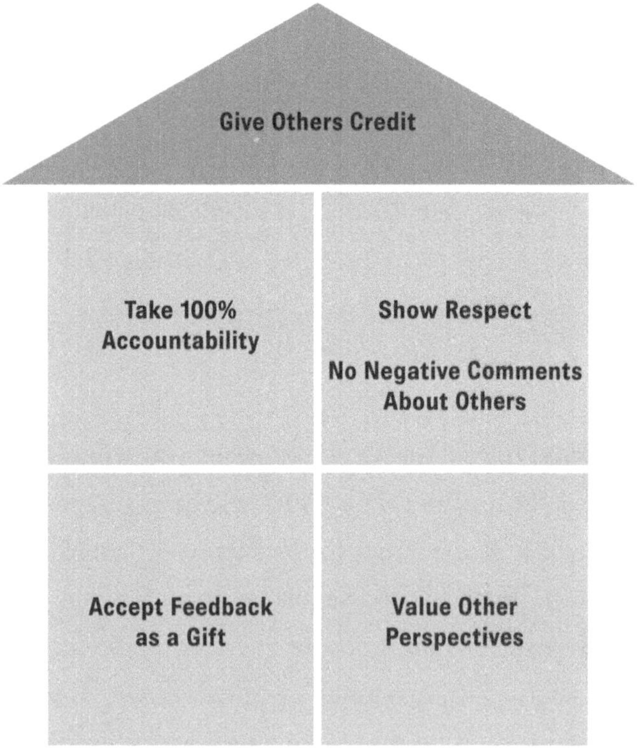

Why is this crucial for CEOs and their top teams? Ego talk prevents honest, constructive conversations, resulting in team conflicts, board issues, and, tragically, even CEOs getting fired, losing major customers and business partners, going through divorces, or losing relationships with their kids.

To master your ego, my top ego-parking tip is simple: When in a negative emotional state, do not make decisions, solve problems, or communicate with other human beings, because you are guaranteed to be in ego talk and you will have deep regrets about how you show up. Don't pick up the phone, don't send an email, and don't talk to another human being until you get yourself into a positive emotional state. If possible, use the twenty-four-hour rule so you can avoid reacting to the situation and can prepare to respond when you are in the house of leadership. Recognize that your negative thoughts and feelings aren't always the truth; much suffering arises from believing them. Instead, shift into your positive brain or, in the words of game changer Shirzad Chamine, your "sage brain."[11] This involves daily practices such as positive intelligence breathing and mindfulness to calm the mind and get access to your creative, inspired, positive brain so you can show up as an inspired leader rather than an ego-talk leader. If you are not able to buy time and use the twenty-four-hour rule, you can use the following technique in the moment:

Stop.

Breathe in and breathe out, and use the mantra of *calm down*. Do the above three times and then ask yourself these questions:

1. How am I feeling? If you're still in a negative emotional state, ask to reschedule the meeting.

---

11 Ibid.

2. Am I in the house of ego or the house of leadership? If you're not in the house of leadership, ask to reschedule the meeting.
3. What needs to happen now? Only respond when you are in the house of leadership.

The ego, in its unmastered state, tends to behave in predictable ways, especially when we are in a negative emotional state—feeling angry, annoyed, frustrated, stressed, or freaked out. I always ask myself—and encourage those I coach to ask themselves—*Am I showing up as the best version of myself?* The house of leadership is where we are the best version of ourselves. When someone from your top team shows up in the house of ego, instead of judging them and making them wrong, help them shift to the house of leadership by sharing your experience of how you do it on a daily basis. Our members share the concepts of the *house of ego* and the *house of leadership* with their top teams so they can all be on the ego mastery journey together.

During the tumultuous early days of the pandemic, the pressures were immense, and sometimes, my own ego threatened to derail critical relationships. I distinctly remember a difficult phone call with my board chair. We were at an impasse over a strategic direction, and my frustration was mounting. Internally, my judge—that critical, fear-based part of my brain that I also call the ego—was getting incredibly loud. My ego urged me to prioritize being right over being effective.

In that moment of intense negative emotion, my mind raced with all the things I wanted to say, the justifications, the counterarguments. It was a clear internal battle, as my ego urged me to react impulsively and not show up as the best version of myself. I constantly remind myself, and the CEOs I coach, that when you're in an angry, frustrated, or stressed-out state, you absolutely should not communicate with another human being—especially your board chair.

We ended the call abruptly, as I had another meeting to attend. Later that day, I had time to reflect on what had happened and why I showed up in ego talk with my board chair. I recognized that my thoughts were not necessarily the truth, and that my ego was trying to make me suffer by focusing on judgment—judging myself, judging my board chair, and judging the circumstances as bad. This self-awareness was the first step in parking my ego.

I was then able to shift from ego talk and the desire to be right to being a more caring, vulnerable, assertive human being (house of leadership).

I reached out to book a follow-up call with my board chair. Instead of getting defensive, I chose to show up in a way that would preserve trust in the relationship and help us come up with an aligned strategic direction. At the start of the phone call, I said, "Hey, I did not show up as the best version of myself, and I want to apologize." He replied, "I want to apologize too, as I did not show up as the best version of myself either, so let's start over and let go of the previous conversation." We were able to work together to come up with an aligned strategic direction. We both felt good about our relationship and the decision we made together that would result in significant growth during challenging times.

It's a daily, ongoing success habit to park my ego, quiet my judge, and show up as the best version of myself in the house of leadership. And when I do slip up—because it's not possible to be at 100 percent all the time—the immediate response is to apologize, owning my part rather than blaming others. This personal journey continually reinforces my belief that for CEOs and their top teams, mastering one's ego is a fundamental leadership skill, not just for business success but for profound personal well-being and strong relationships across all aspects of life.

Daily Success Habits

Building ego mastery involves consistent daily practices that help you become aware of your ego and gently guide yourself toward a more positive and inspired state.

HABIT #1: HOUSE OF EGO SELF-ASSESSMENT

To measure your progress in ego mastery, you can use a simple self-assessment tool, rating yourself on a scale of 0 to 10 on how defensive you tend to be, how much you play the blame game, and how often you make other people wrong and criticize them. This provides a practical way to gauge your current patterns and track improvement. Regularly checking in with yourself about these ego-driven behaviors helps you become more self-aware. In difficult conversations, when you notice yourself in ego talk, you can stop and apologize in the moment to minimize the damage to the relationship and to move things forward in a positive direction. If the other person is in ego talk, you can use MVE (mirror, validate, empathy—explained later in this chapter) to help quiet the other person's ego and move forward in a positive direction.

HABIT #2: EMOTIONAL STATE CHECK-IN

I have shared that my daily routine includes positive intelligence and mindfulness practices. I have found positive intelligence techniques from Shirzad Chamine to be game-changing tools to help master my ego and help CEOs master their egos. These practices, in particular the ten-second PQ reps throughout the day, give me greater access to my positive inspired brain and effectively park my ego and the thousands of negative thoughts swirling in my head. "A PQ Rep is a ten-second hyper-focus on one of your senses. PQ Reps boost your

Self-Command muscle the same way that dumbbell reps would boost your physical body. Doing PQ Reps is a foundational practice for building your Mental Fitness."[12] Ensuring I get my recommended seven to eight hours of sleep each night, as advised by longevity experts, is also vital for maintaining a positive emotional state and managing my emotional responses.

HABIT #3: EGO-PARKING PRACTICE

This is about actively choosing to let go and accept things rather than letting your ego cling to negativity. A key part of this is being able to apologize. It's not humanly possible to park your ego 100 percent of the time, so aiming for 80 percent is a realistic goal. When you catch yourself judging yourself or others, use the empathy practice to step back and ask yourself "How can I help this person?" or "How might I show them some love?" This aligns with the MVE tool kit we'll explore later in the chapter. This practice helps you shift from beating yourself up to giving yourself a pat on the back, fostering a positive inner dialogue. It means taking 100 percent responsibility for your own actions, reactions, and responses to the people around you.

CEO Success Story

I've seen thousands of CEOs transformed by mastering their egos. One particular story stands out—a CEO who was literally on the brink of being fired because of her ego-talk behaviors.

This CEO had a meeting with her board, and she came to me afterward, incredibly defensive and ready to complain about the board, convinced they were horrible people. Her ego was in full fight

12 Mary Sherman, "Positive Intelligence (Revisited)," UVA FEAP, July 2024, https://uvafeap.substack.com/p/positive-intelligence.

mode, preparing for a battle. I used the MVE framework with her, mirroring what she was saying, validating her feelings of frustration, and empathizing by telling her that if I were in her shoes, I would likely feel the same way. This helped her to park her ego so we could have a real and honest discussion about the situation.

The consequences of ego talk for CEOs are immense; it often leads to being fired, facing divorce, or having other important relationships completely break down. It also significantly increases personal stress and anxiety because so many business challenges revolve around people, people, and people.

I guided this CEO through a thirty-day plan designed to prevent her being fired and help her show up as a more inspired leader—the successful CEO she could be. The first step was incredibly difficult for her: She needed to go back and apologize to her board chair and every single board member for her previous ego-talk behavior. This required immense courage and a willingness to acknowledge that her past success and brilliance didn't excuse her current behavior. By taking ownership of her actions and committing to coaching, she began to realize that she was in control of her leadership journey and could inspire herself every day, rather than blaming the board or anyone else. The great news is that several years later, she is still the CEO of this company and she has great relationships with her board and top team, delivering remarkable results. This story powerfully illustrates how mastering ego allows for profound transformation in both our professional and personal lives, leading to stronger relationships, reduced stress, and accelerated business results.

Build Your Mastery

To help you build your ego mastery, I recommend several practical strategies or tools (also illustrated in the diagram):

- **The "shield" technique for not taking things personally:** When someone is expressing anger or frustration, I acknowledge that their negative brain and ego are showing up, not their amazing human being self. My role is to put on my "Teflon shield," reminding myself that their outburst isn't about me; it's about them. In fact, I try to use humor to disarm them, and I find the empathy to see them as a lovable human being, even if they are not so lovable in that moment. My job is to help them get into a positive emotional state. This simple mental shift is incredibly powerful for preventing their negativity from affecting your own emotional state.
- **Using the "no ego" language of the MVE and CVA frameworks:** These frameworks are cornerstones of effective leadership and ego mastery.
- **Use MVE when someone is showing up in a negative emotional state:** It's a tool for you to use to help other people park their ego:
    - **Mirror:** Reflect back what the other person is saying to show you're listening. For example, if a customer is upset and decides to end your relationship, you might say, "So, what I'm hearing you say is that our service has been unacceptable, and you're frustrated because of past issues." Is there more? Keep repeating back exactly what they say until they are finished sharing everything they want to say to you.
    - **Validate:** Acknowledge that their feelings and perspective are understandable given the situation. "It makes sense that you feel this way. We have missed some

delivery dates recently. We're grateful we've resolved our supply chain issue."

  - **Empathize:** Put yourself in their shoes and genuinely express understanding for their emotions. "If I were in your shoes, I would feel the exact same frustration and anger that you're feeling. Regardless of the reason, this impacted you and your people." This process helps the other person park their ego and become more receptive to a constructive conversation. Most people lack these tools, which often leads to conflict and damaged relationships.

- **Use CVA to help you park your own ego and get ready to respond to another person. For example, after you finish using the MVE approach with your customer, respond using the CVA tool:**
  - **Demonstrate That You Care:** "Thank you for sharing your insights with me. You are a really important customer and you matter to me personally, given that we've done business together for so many years."
  - **Show Vulnerability:** "I'm feeling disappointed that you decided to end our business relationship without giving us an opportunity to make things right."
  - **Be Assertive:** "My request is that you give me forty-eight hours to work with my team to come up with a plan to win back your business. Are you prepared to honor my request?"
  - You are more likely to win back your customer by using a no ego MVE and CVA approach than using ego talk.

- **Specific ego management strategies:** Beyond the MVE and CVA, it's vital to recognize that your thoughts and feelings are not always the truth. Much of our suffering comes from believing these thoughts and feelings. Becoming a witness to your thoughts and emotions allows you to observe them without letting them control you. You can then choose to park your ego and step into your positive brain (which, as previously noted, Shirzad Chamine refers to as the "sage brain").

HOUSE OF LEADERSHIP TOOLS

DAILY SUCCESS HABITS

Positive People

Use CVA Demonstrate That You Care Show Vulnerability Be Assertive	Use MVE Mirror (is there more?) Validate (makes sense) Empathy (you feel)
Put Your Shield On	Activate Ego Management Strategies

Deeper Dive

To deepen your understanding of ego mastery, I encourage you to explore the insights of several game changers who have significantly influenced my own journey:

- **Eckhart Tolle:** Reading his book *A New Earth*, in particular chapter 3, was a pivotal moment for me, marking the beginning of my deep understanding of how ego can impede success.[13] *The Power of Now* is another impactful work that explores similar concepts.[14]
- **Michael Singer:** His book *The Untethered Soul* profoundly taught me that our thoughts and feelings are not the truth, and that much suffering arises from believing them. Learning to be a witness to your internal dialogue is a powerful step in this journey. For example, he powerfully reminds readers that they are not their self-concept.[15]
- **Shirzad Chamine:** His work on positive intelligence, particularly the concept of ten-second PQ Reps, provides practical tools for amplifying your positive brain and effectively mastering your ego. He also trains you to develop and tap into your inner sage—essential for intercepting your internal saboteurs.[16]

---

13 Eckhart Tolle, *A New Earth: Awakening to Your Life's Purpose* (Penguin, 2008).

14 Eckhart Tolle, *The Power of Now: A Guide to Spiritual Enlightenment* (New World Library, 1999).

15 Michael A. Singer, *The Untethered Soul: The Journey Beyond Yourself* (New Harbinger Publications, 2007).

16 Shirzad Chamine, *Positive Intelligence: Why Only 20% of Teams and Individuals Achieve Their True Potential and How You Can Achieve Yours* (Greenleaf Book Group Press, 2012).

- **Byron Katie:** Her Four Questions framework is an invaluable tool for challenging stressful thoughts and gaining new perspectives, especially when facing difficult situations.[17] The questions are:

    1. Is it true?
    2. Can you absolutely know that it's true?
    3. How do you react when you believe that thought?
    4. Who would you be without the thought?

  An even more powerful question she poses is, What if the opposite was equally true? For instance, if you believe losing a rock star CFO on your top team is a disaster, considering that it might be the *best* thing for your company can instantly shift your perspective, helping you accept reality and move into an inspired brain. This tool kit is immensely valuable for navigating bad news and reframing challenges.

The impact of ego on decision-making is significant. When leaders are in a negative emotional state, ego talk gets really loud, and it leads to suffering and can result in bad decisions and a lot of wasted time. By mastering the ego, leaders can move into a positive state, allowing for clearer, more resourceful decision-making. The consequences of ego talk, as highlighted by our CEO stories and discussions in peer groups, often manifest as busted relationships, job loss, and increased stress and anxiety.

17 *The Work of Byron Katie*, accessed June 1, 2025, https://thework.com/.

Identify Your Game Changers

In the area of ego mastery, your game changers can come in various forms:

- **Authors and thought leaders:** The individuals I've mentioned—Eckhart Tolle, Michael Singer, Shirzad Chamine, and Byron Katie—are all game changers because they provide proven road maps to success in understanding and managing the ego, and they are willing to share their wisdom through their books and teachings.
- **Peers in confidential peer groups:** Being part of a high-performing CEO peer group means surrounding yourself with real CEOs who are committed to parking their egos and being vulnerable with each other so they can show up as the best versions of themselves. In these groups, you witness and learn how others show up consistently in the house of leadership, never saying anything negative about others and taking ownership of their actions. This positive and inspiring peer learning environment provides constant modeling and support for ego mastery.
- **External CEO coaches and mental fitness coaches:** External CEO coaches and mental fitness coaches can be game changers for you and your top team, providing feedback and specific strategies to help you and your top team on your ego mastery journeys.

END-OF-CHAPTER CHECK-IN

Rate the following on a Likert scale (e.g., 1 = strongly disagree, 5 = strongly agree), and get your score:

EGO MASTERY

- I pause and reflect before responding when I notice strong negative emotions.
- I practice not taking things personally and use empathy in challenging conversations.
- I recognize when my ego is influencing my decisions and take steps to reset.

EGO MASTERY REFLECTION

What recent situation triggered my ego? If I were to relive it with compassion and curiosity, how might the outcome change?

GAME CHANGER PROMPT

Who helps me check my ego without judgment? Who models humility and self-awareness? Who can support me in navigating emotionally charged situations?

CHAPTER 4

EMOTIONAL MASTERY AND MENTAL FITNESS

If your emotional abilities aren't in hand, if you don't have self-awareness, if you are not able to manage your distressing emotions, if you can't have empathy and have effective relationships, then no matter how smart you are, you are not going to get very far.

—DANIEL GOLEMAN

Success in emotional mastery means that CEOs know how to show up in a positive emotional state 80 percent of the time, develop mental fitness, and enjoy the leadership journey moment by moment. This isn't just about feeling good; it's about being effective, resourceful, and inspiring, no matter what challenges come your way.

The core of emotional mastery is becoming self-aware of your emotions. Many people aren't even aware when they are in a negative emotional state, whether they are angry, frustrated, annoyed, stressed out, or freaked out. My number one emotional mastery tip for CEOs is "When you are in a negative emotional state, don't make a decision, pick up the phone, or try to problem-solve." Why? Because you will react instead of responding to situations, and you will say things that you will regret to the people around you. You will also make bad decisions, waste time, and likely damage relationships. When our emotions are negative, our ego gets really loud, leading us to say things that are fear-based or ego-driven, not reflecting our best selves. (Once again—these mastery areas are all interconnected.)

The goal is to learn how to get yourself into a positive emotional state and, ideally, to stay in that state approximately 80 percent of the time. As I have said before, 100 percent emotional mastery is impossible—and making that your goal sets you up for perfectionism and a very critical judge.

When you are in a positive state—happy, excited, enthusiastic, ecstatic, or optimistic—your inspired brain kicks in, enabling you to make better decisions, solve problems more effectively, collaborate effectively, positively impact those around you, and take decisive action.

Emotions are contagious, so if you haven't mastered your own emotions and someone else approaches you in a negative state, you can easily get pulled down with them. This is why I emphasize the You Go First philosophy: Learn to master your own emotions first so you can help others shift from a negative emotional state to a positive emotional state and minimize ego talk. Mental fitness is a leadership tool kit to help you master your emotions (see diagram on page 71).

When we are in a negative emotional state, we go below the line, we start beating ourselves up over past mistakes and catastrophizing potential failures. We lose perspective, causing us to make poor decisions that waste a lot of time. Based on my experience working with CEOs and their top teams, most people typically spend 80 percent of their time below the line and only 20 percent of their time above the line. The key to emotional mastery is to reverse this ratio.

Inspired leaders with strong mental fitness spend 80 percent of their time in a positive emotional state above the line. They make better decisions and are able to solve problems more effectively when they are above the line. People look to top teams to help them get and stay above the line and move forward in a positive direction, especially during challenging times.

	PAST	PRESENT	FUTURE
ABOVE THE LINE	Relive Positive Moments Learn From Mistakes	Maximize Energy Be in the Moment Focus on Empowering Thoughts	Visualize Success Focus on What You Want Focus on Compelling Vision
BELOW THE LINE	Relive Mistakes Worry Guilt Regrets	Minimize Energy Thousands of Thoughts	Visualize Failure Focus on What You Don't Want Worry Fear Anxiety

Our ego/judge keeps us below the line by judging ourselves, other people, and our circumstances, which causes our negative emotional state. The key to getting above the line is to celebrate when you catch your judge in order to quiet it. The key to staying above the line is to practice mental fitness:

1. Ask yourself these powerful questions: What do I want? What does success look like? What is my purpose? If I knew I couldn't fail, what would I do?
2. Use ten-second PQ reps one hundred times a day to access your positive brain. A PQ rep is taking ten seconds at a time to redirect your attention to the now. A rep might be inhaling and exhaling, paying careful attention to the sensation of breathing for ten seconds. You might focus on a different sense, taking ten seconds to shut your eyes and become attuned to the sounds around you—or a far-off sound that is faint. These types of reps are like mini mental training exercises, training your mind to be calmer and more fit.
3. Learn how to (1) love yourself and catch yourself doing things right every day, (2) love every human being (not necessarily all of their behaviors), and (3) love everything in life by treating it all as a gift.

Daily Success Habits

To cultivate emotional mastery and mental fitness, I recommend incorporating several daily habits that reinforce a positive mindset and emotional resilience.

HABIT #1: MASTER EMOTIONS WITH HEALTHY PHYSICAL EXERCISE

The mind and body are closely connected. My goal is to live to 120 with a healthy lifespan and full of the same energy, passion, and inspiration that I have now. That's exactly why I exercise every day, as I have shared. But it's not only that I want to live a long life. I know that daily exercise will help me live a happy life—and help with my emotional state and mental fitness.

This is backed by science. For example, in a Harvard Health article, researchers "saw a 26% decrease in odds for becoming depressed for each major increase in objectively measured physical activity. … This increase in physical activity is what you might see on your activity tracker if you replaced 15 minutes of sitting with 15 minutes of running, or one hour of sitting with one hour of moderate activity like brisk walking."[18]

HABIT #2: STRESS-REDUCTION TECHNIQUES

Developing effective daily stress-reduction techniques is fundamental to emotional mastery. One powerful tool I use and recommend is mindfulness. I've learned various meditation and mindfulness tools over the years, and they are crucial for amplifying the positive brain and becoming more resourceful and positive daily.

A specific technique I employ is the 4-7-8 breathing exercise. You breathe in for four seconds, hold for seven seconds, and then breathe out for eight seconds. This can be done subtly, even in the middle of a challenging meeting, to ground yourself and neutralize negative emotions. It shifts you from a reactive ego state—wanting to

---

18 Harvard Health Publishing, "More Evidence That Exercise Can Boost Mood," *Harvard Health Publishing*, May 1, 2019, https://www.health.harvard.edu/mind-and-mood/more-evidence-that-exercise-can-boost-mood.

blame or get defensive—to a more present and grounded one. Though popularized more recently, it has its roots in ancient yogic practices.[19]

Another strategy is to buy yourself time before reacting to bad news or negative interactions. If you receive a triggering email or someone approaches you in a negative emotional state and you can't immediately get into a positive state, excuse yourself. You might say, "Let's take some time to reflect on this and regroup later today or tomorrow," or "Let's get some more facts before we meet again." This prevents you from responding from an ego-driven place and allows you to prepare for a more constructive interaction.

Finally, posture plays a role. When people are in a negative emotional state, they often slump or have closed-off body language. By consciously adopting an open, confident posture, you can influence your internal state, moving toward positivity. By the way, I've had a standing desk for about ten years and I never sit down when I'm working in my home office. This has been a game-changing strategy to help me master my emotions and to maximize my energy every day.

HABIT #3: CATCH YOURSELF AND YOUR TOP TEAM DOING THINGS RIGHT EVERY DAY

Catching yourself and your top team doing things right every day is the practice of patting yourself on the back every day and consistently focusing on your accomplishments and strengths using a 5:1 ratio of positive to negative self-feedback. When you make a mistake, accept that you made a mistake and let it go. Or take some time to reflect and learn from the mistake to avoid future mistakes. If you go first using this approach to emotional mastery, you'll be able to use the same 5:1 ratio of positivity/negativity with your top team when dealing

19 "How to Do the 478 Breathing Exercise," *Cleveland Clinic*, September 6, 2022, https://health.clevelandclinic.org/4-7-8-breathing.

with their mistakes to keep everyone in a positive emotional state 80 percent of the time. In most organizations, feedback often focuses on weaknesses and areas for improvement. Emotional mastery involves building on your strengths and your top team's strengths. This means intentionally spending your time in areas where you excel, enabling you to make the biggest possible contribution. The same approach applies to your top team.

By regularly acknowledging your strengths and successes, you build self-confidence and maintain a positive emotional state. This approach serves as a continuous reminder of your capabilities and positive impact, countering the inner critic—your judge—and external negativity that might chip away at your self-esteem.

CEO Success Story

I've had the privilege of coaching thousands of CEOs, and one story powerfully illustrates the impact of low CEO emotional mastery.

I was once doing an in-person coaching session with a new CEO client. As I walked by his assistant's desk, she stopped me and pointed to a stoplight on her desk. It had three colors: red, yellow, and green. She explained that when the light was red, no one, not even his family, was allowed to bother him. When it was yellow, she could interrupt him, but only if absolutely necessary. And when it was green, he was open to interruptions. This system, she told me, was how she managed his calendar and kept him from blowing up at people. Given that the stoplight was yellow, I asked his EA for permission to proceed with my coaching session.

I started the coaching session by asking the CEO, "How are you doing today?"

He said he was having a really bad day (it was only ten in the morning) because they had lost their biggest customer, his board chair was really upset with him, and his CFO was late delivering the draft board package for him to review prior to submitting it to the board.

I expressed that I was sorry to hear about all of his challenges. I asked, "I'm curious, is this how you show up when other people come into your office?"

He said, "I'm the CEO, and people need to realize I'm under a lot of pressure. They need to adjust to my style and understand that I have a lot of challenges." To me, this was a clear sign that he lacked self-awareness regarding his emotional state and its impact on others.

I told him that if he was up for it, I'd advise that he start our coaching program. I told him, "This way, going forward, you can show up in a positive emotional state when people come to your office. You'll enjoy the CEO journey a lot more, and you'll be able to inspire your top team to show up in a positive emotional state with their top teams. This is how you will avoid losing your top customers in the future, and you'll be able to more effectively deal with your board chair and your CFO.

He said, "I'm up for it! I'm not having a lot of fun, and there must be a better way for me to lead this company into the future."

As I was leaving that session, I invited his EA to join our next meeting, so she could come in and let the CEO know that she had been using the stoplight to manage his calendar. She was terrified, fearing she would get fired. I reassured her, "No, I promise you won't get fired. We're going to talk this through, and he needs your help." I emphasized that we all need help from others—peers, EAs, coaches, mentors, significant others, kids—to help us learn how to master our emotions.

In the subsequent meeting, the EA bravely told the CEO about the stoplight system. His reaction was transformative. He stated that he had been working with me and was committed to improving. He apologized for his past behavior and gave full permission for his EA and top team to stop him if he messed up in the future. He showed a complete shift because he *wanted* to change and was open to learning new tools.

This CEO's story highlights that emotional mastery isn't about being perfect but about self-awareness, being a lifelong learner, and a willingness to change. It also demonstrates that it's not that difficult to shift your emotional state once you become aware and committed.

Build Your Mastery

Building emotional mastery involves specific frameworks and techniques that help you navigate your thoughts and feelings in a constructive way.

PROCESS FOR RECOGNIZING AND ELIMINATING STRESSFUL THOUGHTS

The key to recognizing and managing stressful thoughts is to realize that your thoughts and feelings are not always the truth. We have thousands of thoughts a day, and our ego often infuses these with negativity that can lead to suffering. (Our judge wants us to be miserable!)

If you believe a stressful thought—for example, *This is horrible* or *I'll never be successful*—you will feel negative emotions. The mind is powerful: If you think something is bad, you'll be in a negative emotional state; if you think it's great, you'll be positive.

The process isn't about *eliminating* thoughts entirely, which isn't possible, but about becoming aware that they are not necessarily factual. This awareness allows you to become a witness to your thoughts and feelings. Instead of letting them control you, you can observe them and say, *OK, that's my judge*, or *That's just my negative brain*, or *That is my fear brain talking*.

Once you've gained this awareness, you can use techniques such as Byron Katie's four questions from the ego mastery chapter to challenge the thought, or simply focus on what success looks like, what you want, and your purpose. This helps you to park your ego and step into your inspired brain, or sage brain, where you can show up in a positive emotional state and make better decisions.

Deeper Dive

In this deeper dive, I'd like to share insights from various thought leaders who have significantly influenced my understanding and application of emotional mastery.

RELEVANT RESEARCH ON EMOTIONAL INTELLIGENCE, GRIT, AND MENTAL FITNESS

My work with CEOs consistently reinforces the importance of emotional intelligence and mental fitness. I speak about mental fitness as one of the fundamental CEO leadership skills of personal mastery, meaning how I inspire myself every day, my health, and how I show up every day. Taking care of myself, my health, and my mental fitness allows me to show up as the best version of myself and have more love to give to the world.

Emotional intelligence is about being aware of your own emotions and the emotions of others and then using that awareness to guide your thinking and behavior. When CEOs fail to master their emotions, it leads to damaged relationships, divorces, partnerships breaking up, and even getting fired. It is truly heartbreaking to see these consequences when CEOs don't have the tools to master their emotions effectively. Here I will add—emotional mastery and ego mastery are especially entwined. The ego can rear its head and incite the emotions to be defensive, angry, blaming, etc.

Steve Foran's book *Surviving to Thriving: The 10 Laws of Grateful Leadership* focuses on the power of gratitude. He writes, "Make a list of what you're grateful for ... Read or listen to what others are grateful for .... Share your gratitudes with others .... Say thank you."[20] Daily gratitude journaling is a powerful tool to shift your emotional state away from stress and anxiety. Foran says it's the key to truly thriving. This aligns perfectly with the principles of emotional mastery, as a mindset of appreciation helps foster a positive emotional state necessary for effective leadership.

By understanding that external circumstances and even internal thoughts are not definitive truths, you can choose how to respond, rather than simply reacting. This perspective is vital for maintaining emotional mastery and clarity as a leader.

Identify Your Game Changers

No leader can achieve emotional mastery alone. It requires a strategic approach to identifying and leveraging game changers.

EMOTIONAL INTELLIGENCE MENTORS

Emotional intelligence mentors can be found within your existing network or sought out specifically for their expertise in mastering emotions. These could be peers, trusted advisors, or even coaches.

20 Steve Foran, *Surviving to Thriving: 10 Laws of Grateful Leadership* (Calvin Simpson, 2019).

When you find yourself in a negative emotional state and can't get out of it, reaching out to someone you trust is crucial. They can help you process what's happening and guide you back into a positive emotional state, acting as a sounding board and offering constructive perspectives. Structured peer support forums can provide this kind of assistance, offering a confidential space where CEOs can talk about everything—business, family, and personal—without competitors in the room. This diverse team of fourteen peers can help you navigate life's bumps and emotional challenges.

SUPPORT OF MENTAL HEALTH PROFESSIONALS

It's vital to acknowledge that sometimes emotional challenges go beyond what self-coaching or peer support can address. In such cases, I strongly encourage seeking the support of mental health professionals. My approach is always judgment-free. If I discover a CEO has an addiction or bullying issues or is struggling with severe mental health challenges that are beyond my coaching expertise, I refer them to specialists. There are times when medication or specialized therapy is necessary, and professional help, combined with coaching and peer support, creates a comprehensive approach to well-being.

STRATEGIC VALUE OF SUPPORT NETWORK MEMBERS

Your broader support network plays a strategic role in maintaining emotional mastery. This includes your board, your top team, advisors, friends, and family. Your top-twenty people you love! When you feel lonely at the top and something goes wrong, reminding yourself that you have these game changers around you is essential. Surrounding yourself with these individuals is fundamental to relationship mastery and prevents the isolation that can amplify negative emotions.

In the MacKay CEO Forums, we foster a culture in which CEOs are challenged to identify who is on their top-twenty list of relationships they need to build or deepen. This strategic focus ensures that leaders intentionally cultivate a network of game changers—whether board members, mentors, or peer group connections—who can provide invaluable emotional and practical support.

By diligently applying these tools and leveraging your game changers, you will not only gain profound emotional mastery but also cultivate a deep self-awareness that empowers you to inspire yourself every day. This foundational internal mastery is the first step in creating a lasting positive impact on your top team and your organization.

END-OF-CHAPTER CHECK-IN

Rate the following on a Likert scale (e.g., 1 = strongly disagree, 5 = strongly agree), and get your score:

EMOTIONAL MASTERY

- I maintain a gratitude practice that helps me stay grounded and positive.
- I can shift my emotional state quickly when stress or resentment shows up.
- I reflect on and question stressful thoughts instead of letting them control me.

EMOTIONAL MASTERY REFLECTION

What's a recurring stressful thought I carry? What if the opposite were just as true?

GAME CHANGER PROMPT

Who supports my emotional well-being? Who helps me shift perspective, stay present, or cultivate resilience?

CHAPTER 5 PROACTIVE HEALTH MASTERY

It's never too late to be healthy.

—KEVIN BRADY

For decades, I've had the profound privilege of working with thousands of CEOs and executives. What I've seen, time and again, is a consistent pattern: These brilliant, driven leaders, who excel at navigating complex business challenges and building thriving companies, often struggle profoundly with one critical area—their personal health and well-being. It's a silent crisis in the C-suite, and it's heartbreaking to witness. Many CEOs tragically do not make their mental and physical health their number one priority, leading to burnout, severe health diagnoses, and even divorce. This is why, in the MacKay Mastery Model, we say that dead CEOs don't meet their targets. It's a stark reality but one that drives home the absolute necessity of proactive health mastery.

My definition of success in this area, and indeed in life, is maximizing your individual productivity so you can make the biggest contribution in all areas. And that starts with your mental and physical health. My personal goal is to live to 120 with a healthy lifespan and then go boom!

Truly, my goal is healthy longevity with sustained energy, mental fitness, and purpose. This isn't just a whimsical aspiration; it's a deeply intentional life goal that anchors my daily choices.

My journey toward this audacious goal began about eight years ago, when I attended a Singularity University program. There, I had the privilege of meeting visionaries such as Ray Kurzweil and Peter Diamandis, who are true game changers in the field of longevity. It was a pivotal moment. I realized that with the exponential changes and advancements in medical technology, living to 120 (and even beyond) with a healthy lifespan was not just a dream but a genuine possibility. This revelation profoundly shifted my mindset from a passive "we'll see" approach to an active "I am going to set this goal and tell the world" commitment.

I then brought this mindset back to MacKay CEO Forums because, as I said, most CEOs don't take care of their health. I felt a responsibility to be an exemplar, not just for my own family and our MacKay community but for the thousands of CEOs I coach. If I don't go first, if I don't prioritize my own health, how can I authentically encourage others to do the same? This is the very essence of the You Go First philosophy that underpins our entire MacKay Mastery Model.

The Common Pitfalls: Why CEOs Struggle with Health

The single biggest barrier I hear from CEOs when it comes to prioritizing their health is, "I don't have time." This mindset is deeply entrenched. Those caught in the 24/7 trap are spinning and moving at great speed—usually without a thought for their health.

This often leads to neglecting crucial preventative measures, such as daily mental and physical fitness, annual physicals, colonoscopies, and MRI screenings, and even failing to address pain or suffering, because the mindset of many at the top is to simply push through it. The stark reality is, this neglect leads to tragic consequences, such as severe health diagnoses that could have been prevented with earlier detection.

Beyond the perceived lack of time, another significant pitfall is fear. CEOs, like many people, fear getting a bad diagnosis, thus leading to medical avoidance. They often prefer to not know what might be lurking, operating under the dangerous illusion that ignorance is bliss. But I constantly challenge this. If you do know, you can actually do something about it. Early detection, even of something as serious as cancer, can be lifesaving. The fear is an ego-driven response, a part of our negative brain that wants us to catastrophize and believe the worst.

Finally, the ego also plays a role in preventing CEOs from being vulnerable and seeking help. There's often a deeply ingrained belief that a CEO must be the smartest person in the room, have all the answers, and never show weakness. This can make it incredibly difficult for them to admit they're struggling, to delegate, or to ask for support, compounding their stress-related health issues.

Daily Success Habits for Proactive Health Mastery

Health mastery is not a one-time fix; it's a daily discipline. It requires intentional, consistent effort every single day to ensure you are showing up as the best version of yourself.

HABIT #1: ONE-HOUR DAILY COMMITMENT TO FOCUS ON HEALTH AND WELL-BEING

The biggest myth I work to debunk is the I-don't-have-time mindset. The reality we have emphasized in this book is you have twenty-four hours in a day, and after getting the recommended seven to eight hours of sleep, you have approximately one hundred waking hours a week. The key is to be strategic and intentional about how you spend that time and whom you spend it with.

This means that blocking time in your calendar for your mental and physical health is nonnegotiable. Your meetings with your board are blocked in your calendar. No one cancels those. And your health is even more important. Blocking time will look different for every CEO. Whether it's for exercise, mental fitness, personal trainers, or healthy meals, it needs to be scheduled like any other critical business meeting.

As previously stated, the best times for self-care for me are first thing in the morning and before bed at night. This sets my entire day up for success, allowing me to access my inspired brain and diminish the impact of my negative brain. I was heartened twenty years ago when I read the book *Younger Next Year* (a game changer for me), which makes clear that what you do today directly impacts your future health and longevity.[21]

HABIT #2: PRIORITIZING QUALITY SLEEP

I've discussed that sleep deprivation is a genuine crisis among CEOs. Many boast about how little sleep they need, but this is a recipe for disaster. If you're not getting the recommended seven to eight hours of sleep, your brain is not functioning effectively, you're accelerating your aging process, and you won't be an effective decision-maker.

---

21 Chris Crowley and Henry S. Lodge, *Younger Next Year: Live Strong, Fit, Sexy, and Smart—Until You're 80 and Beyond* (Workman Publishing, 2019).

I tell CEOs to literally block sleep time in their calendar. If you're struggling to achieve this, it's crucial to seek expert help, whether it's a doctor or a sleep specialist, to address the underlying challenges. (And for that matter, if your significant other is complaining about your snoring, get a sleep expert to help you.) Your health cannot afford for you to ignore this fundamental need.

HABIT #3: USE TEN-SECOND PQ REPS ONE HUNDRED TIMES A DAY FOR MENTAL FITNESS

I've mentioned a game-changing tool for building positive intelligence. It's a simple, effective technique that involves ten-second PQ reps throughout the day. When I'm working out with my personal trainers, I'm often asked/told to do ten reps for bicep curls. My positive intelligence coach, Joe Heraldo, asked/told me to do ten-second PQ reps one hundred times a day. At first, it sounded like a crazy thing to do. However, after twenty-one days of doing ten-second PQ reps one hundred times a day (starting with twelve minutes of PQ reps each morning), I noticed that my stress and anxiety had disappeared, I had much greater access to my positive brain, and I was a lot happier with myself, the people around me, and everything in my life. Mental fitness is not about becoming a meditation guru but about quickly grounding yourself, calming your nervous system, and accessing your inspired brain. Mental fitness requires a personalized approach and a daily discipline just like physical fitness. Whether it's daily PQ reps, meditation, or breathing techniques, getting grounded and fully present in the moment will give you the ability to control your thoughts and feelings so you can respond instead of react to the people and circumstances around you.

Leveraging Your Health Mastery Game Changers

To truly master your health, you need to be proactive and leverage the best resources available. This means having a mindset of constantly seeking game changers for your mental and physical health.

Here's how I apply this to health and how I coach others:

Executive health prevention programs: These programs are an absolute baseline requirement for any high-performing CEO. They typically involve a thorough half-day annual or biannual check-up that goes far beyond a basic physical. They cover a full spectrum of health domains—mental well-being, physical health, cardiovascular status, and other physiological markers. The goal isn't just to catch problems early but to establish a comprehensive diagnostic baseline that can be tracked over time. This enables highly personalized, proactive health recommendations. For busy executives constantly under pressure, these programs are not a luxury—they are a necessity for sustaining long-term performance, energy, and focus. Not only that, most CEOs understand that getting it done in one day is a massive time and energy saver as opposed to coordinating multiple appointments over weeks and months.

Functional health and longevity doctors: This field has emerged as one of the most essential, yet often neglected, aspects of modern executive health. Unlike traditional medicine, which tends to focus on treating illness, functional health and longevity specialists emphasize prevention, optimization, and long-term vitality. In addition to my traditional medicine family doctor, Dr. Bal Pawa, cofounder of Westcoast Women's Clinic in Vancouver, is my integrative health/functional doctor, and she has been a game changer for me over the past decade. She is a world expert in women's health, and she has helped me reframe health not just as the absence of disease but as the presence of optimal energy, resilience, and purpose. Every CEO should explore this growing field of longevity and functional medicine in addition to traditional medicine to achieve proactive health mastery.

Advanced diagnostics: We're living in an era in which diagnostic tools are advancing at a remarkable exponential pace. The technologies now available allow us to peer into our bodies with incredible precision and catch disease at its earliest, most treatable stages. Personally, over the past decade, I've invested in full-body MRI scans and advanced AI-enabled heart screenings (and talked my husband into doing the same, because I want him to live to 120 with a healthy lifespan too). These tools go far beyond the traditional medical check-up. So many CEOs in our MacKay community, for instance, discovered serious health issues through a full-body MRI and were able to get treatments that saved their lives because of early detection. Yes, it can be scary and uncomfortable to confront what might be wrong—but knowledge is power, and early detection saves lives. We must shift from "I don't have time" and fear of getting bad health news to proactive health mastery. And we must inspire our top teams to do the same.

Health navigation companies: Our healthcare system is notoriously complex, fragmented, and difficult to navigate—especially when you're facing something serious. That's where health navigation companies come in. Organizations such as Advica Health, led by our long-term member and innovator partner Kevin Brady, serve as advocates, guides, and game changers within this maze. They connect you and fast-track you to the right specialists, help interpret complicated medical reports, coordinate appointments, and ensure nothing falls through the cracks. They act as your personal health operations team. As a CEO, having this kind of support structure allows you to stay focused on your business while knowing your health is being expertly managed.

Seeking second and third opinions: This is one of my nonnegotiables when it comes to health. The truth is that medicine is both an art and a science, and even the best doctors can have blind spots. I've seen numerous CEOs receive dramatically different diagnoses and treatment plans depending on which expert they consulted. That's why I always encourage people to get a second—and if needed, a third or even fourth—opinion, particularly when dealing with serious or life-altering conditions. You can't outsource your health entirely. As CEOs, we take full ownership of business strategy, and we must apply that same mindset to our own well-being. Doctors offer expertise, but we must remember that we need to be the CEO of our own health. Challenge assumptions, ask questions, and get a second opinion every time you get bad health news!

Nutritionists and fitness coaches: For CEOs who are constantly on the move, it can be extremely difficult to stay on top of healthy habits. Too many airplanes and hotels, things grabbed on the go—or meals forgotten in an intense day. That's where the support of a skilled nutritionist or fitness coach becomes invaluable. Nutritionists can help tailor your diet to your specific health goals, energy needs, and even travel schedule. They provide structure and planning to make healthy eating realistic and sustainable. Fitness coaches play a similar role—creating personalized programs that align with your time constraints, physical limitations, and performance goals. More importantly, they provide accountability, which is critical for consistency. Whether I like it or not—I'm accountable to my various personal trainers and coaches (and most of the time, I love it!).

CEO Success Stories

It is so important to emphasize that the principles in this chapter can transform lives.

One powerful example involves a fifty-year-old CEO I coached who was experiencing panic attacks for the first time in his life. He had pushed himself too hard, neglecting his mental well-being. He wasn't getting enough sleep, he was traveling extensively, and he was drinking too much to manage his stress. My advice was twofold: First, see a doctor to understand the physiological aspects, and second, implement positive intelligence practices. With support from his doctor, and by learning this game-changing positive intelligence tool kit, he learned to manage his negative brain and access his inspired brain. The happy outcome was not only his physical recovery, eliminating his panic attacks, but a profound shift in his leadership approach, achieved by reducing his stress and becoming more inspiring to his team. As CEOs increasingly understand the importance of mental fitness for their top teams, they must go first and take care of their own mental fitness.

Another deeply impactful story is that of a female CEO member of our community who proactively underwent full-body MRI screening. This wasn't because she had symptoms but because she was committed to proactive health. The screening detected early-stage cancer, which was then successfully treated. She has been incredibly vocal in sharing her story within our community, urging others to prioritize early detection, emphasizing that it saved her life. These stories aren't just anecdotes; they are proof that prioritizing health isn't just about personal well-being—it's about the very ability to continue leading, to continue making an impact, and frankly, to continue living a healthy life and inspiring your top team to follow your lead.

Then there have been the *many* burnout stories. Sometimes, sadly, it takes a huge wake-up call—a heart attack or cancer—to make a CEO sit up and realize it's time to take their health seriously.

The Power of Peer Influence and Support Systems

While individual commitment is paramount, no CEO thrives in isolation. A critical aspect of proactive health mastery is leveraging your support network, particularly the power of peer influence within confidential groups like MacKay CEO Forums.

When CEOs sit around a boardroom table with fourteen peers, they hear real stories—the good, the bad, and the ugly. They hear about peers who neglected their health and faced dire consequences, expressing deep regrets. But they also hear about those who, through intentional effort, are running half-marathons, working with functional doctors, and actively pursuing longevity goals. This direct, vulnerable sharing among equals is far more impactful than any doctor's advice or book. Emotions are contagious, and when you surround yourself with peers who are passionate about their health, that positive energy becomes infectious. At a recent peer group meeting, more than half of the CEOs in the room shared in their personal/health updates that they wanted to lose ten pounds. At the end of the meeting, one of the CEOs put a ninety-day challenge out to his peers for all of them to commit to losing ten pounds. All but one of the CEOs joined the ninety-day challenge. One of the CEOs said, "It's summertime; I'm planning to enjoy my summer and then I'll do the ninety-day challenge!" We all had a good chuckle and were grateful for his honesty. I was inspired by the power of peer support to help CEOs achieve proactive health mastery.

Spouses/significant others also play a key role as accountability partners, especially when it comes to sustaining long-term commitments to health and wellness. Their presence in a CEO's personal life makes them uniquely positioned to notice when things are off track, provide encouragement when motivation dips, and celebrate progress along the way. Because of this, we invite spouses to our annual retreats and health-focused presentations, not as passive observers but as active participants. They can be powerful allies—reinforcing healthy habits at home, helping recalibrate when stress or travel disrupts routines, and serving as a steady source of emotional support. In many cases, having a spouse on board can be the difference between a short-term burst of motivation and a truly sustainable lifestyle shift. By including them in these conversations, we strengthen the likelihood that the mindset and practices discussed in our forums translate into real, daily behavioral change.

Ultimately, building a diverse support network—including health professionals, fitness coaches, and accountability partners—is essential to making your health your number one priority. They can challenge you to take 100 percent responsibility for your well-being. Remember, it doesn't have to be lonely at the top when you surround yourself with game changers, especially when it comes to your health.

Also note that proactive health mastery is deeply intertwined with other mastery areas. Your physical and mental health directly impacts your emotional mastery (showing up in a positive emotional state), your mental toughness (resilience and focus), and even your time mastery (having the energy and clarity to be productive). It's a holistic approach to leadership and life for you and your top team.

Inspiring Yourself to Inspire Others

The core message of the MacKay Mastery Model is You Go First. This is profoundly true for proactive health mastery. Prioritizing your health is not selfish; it is the most unselfish thing you can do. When you take care of yourself—your physical health, your mental fitness, your emotional well-being—you show up as the best version of yourself. You have more energy, more clarity, and more love to give the rest of the world.

My dream is to populate the world with inspiring leaders. This starts with each CEO making a deep, personal commitment to their own health mastery. By doing so, you not only transform your own life, but you become a powerful exemplar for your family, your top team, and your entire organization. You break the cycle of burnout and overcome the mental health crisis, and you take a stand on business as a force for good by being committed to the well-being of all of your employees.

END-OF-CHAPTER CHECK-IN

Rate the following on a Likert scale (e.g., 1 = strongly disagree, 5 = strongly agree), and get your score:

PROACTIVE HEALTH MASTERY

- I invest at least one hour a day in activities that support my mental and physical health.
- I proactively use preventative health screenings and wellness services.
- I track habits such as sleep, movement, and nutrition to support long-term vitality.

PROACTIVE HEALTH MASTERY REFLECTION

What's one small shift I could make this week to radically improve my energy and well-being?

GAME CHANGER PROMPT

Who prioritizes their health and models that commitment? Who can help me navigate new health habits or resources?

CHAPTER 6
RELATIONSHIP MASTERY

We cannot control a relationship. We can only contribute to a relationship. All relationships, business or personal, are an opportunity to serve another human being.
—SIMON SINEK

Simon Sinek's quote is true. We cannot control a relationship; instead we can control our part in it. You Go First is about mastering the relationship with yourself. This enables you to show up as the best version of yourself every day before you interact with other people.

This area of the MacKay Mastery Model involves mastering the relationships that truly matter. At an individual level, this means mastering the relationship you have with yourself first and foremost. If that relationship is not inspiring, none of the rest of your relationships will be.

You also must master the relationships with those who are most important to you—your spouse/partner, kids, parents, family, and friends. I call taking care of these most important relationships self-care and family care. Then, as a CEO, mastering business relationships involves surrounding yourself with the right types of people, those who can help you succeed and can support you on your mastery journey. Business is fundamentally about people, and relationship mastery provides the necessary tool kit for this. In this chapter, you will learn that success in this area means being strategic about who is on your "top-twenty business list" of relationships that you need to be building or deepening at any given time, as well as a variety of habits and techniques that you can use to achieve mastery in all your relationships (including the one with yourself).

The Top Twenty: Mastering Key Business Relationships

Do you have a top-twenty list of people you love—not including friends and family? I'm assuming that you love your spouse/partner and most of your friends and family. But what about in your business life? For example, your top-twenty business list can include your board members, your top team, your customers, your peer group, your business partners, and your external advisors.

Business is about people.

Relationship mastery is about treating every person as a human being and with respect. With respect means never judging, criticizing, or saying anything negative about anyone. Relationship mastery is about loving every human being—not necessarily all of their behaviors. And that includes those in our professional life (we'll share our definition of business love in a moment).

Let's be honest, we don't always show up as the best version of ourselves, and the same is true for the people around us. The best version of ourselves is a CVA human being. When we are in a negative emotional state, we show up as the opposite—judging ourselves and judging others, playing the blame game, getting defensive, focusing on being right, and caring more about looking good (house of ego).

If you don't love your top-twenty business list, you won't be successful as a CEO. You might even get fired or pushed out of the business if you damage key strategic relationships, because your ego gets in the way of your ability to build positive relationships with the people around you. I have seen it happen far too many times.

I will never forget one of the founder CEOs I was coaching who said, "I don't love my customers!"

Ryan went on, "In fact, I hate my customers; they don't pay their bills on time, they get into fights with my employees, they have unrealistic expectations, and I spend my days with my team complaining about our customers. I think it's time for me to sell my business and be done with it."

He complained about his top team letting him down. His business partner wasn't, according to Ryan, pulling his weight. I probed, "OK. What about you? Are you showing up as the best version of yourself every day and contributing to the success of the business?"

He readily admitted he wasn't—and the same could be said of how he was showing up at home. Unsurprisingly, the business was suffering as well.

I challenged him, "What if you learned how to love yourself and your top-twenty list of businesspeople? And what if you learned how to park your ego so you can stop blaming everyone around you and you can start showing up as an inspired CEO and your best self?"

I asked for his patience, and I explained my definition of business love:

1. **Openhearted:** Treat every person as a human being and with respect (including yourself). This means showing up as a CVA human being and never saying anything negative about

anyone ever! It also means celebrating your own personal wins every day, whether they are big or small.

2. **Tell the truth:** If you love someone, you tell them the truth. For example, in the case of the CEO I was coaching, I told him, "You can tell your customers that you need them to pay their bills on time and to show respect to your employees. In the case of your business partner, tell the truth about what you need from him. Clarify your expectations with each person on your top team so they can either push back or accept your challenge to them."
3. **Unconditional:** Love them even if they leave you/you leave them. Customers who are not aligned with your core values need to go somewhere else. The same is true for your top team and your business partner. You can wish them all the best whether they are a fit for you or not and even help them find other places to go.

After initially resisting (vehemently), the CEO responded, "This is the last day that I'm going to ever say anything negative about my customers (or anyone else)."

He left with a whole new approach to relationship mastery and showing up as an inspired CEO. Over the next ninety days, he met with every customer, and although 20 percent of the business's customers had to be transitioned out of the business, he was able to generate 50 percent new business from the remaining 80 percent of customers because he showed up with love. He realized that two of his six top team members were not a fit for his business, so he came up with a plan to transition them off the team. He hired an external relationship coach to help him turn his relationship with his business partner around so they could get back on track to grow the business. His family relationships improved as well.

What about you? Are you showing up with your top-twenty business list like Ryan did before he learned how to park his ego and quiet his judge so he could show up as an inspired CEO?

My challenge to you, if you want to take your success to the next level, is to show up like the inspired Ryan and show the love to the people around you (including your spouse and friends/family).

Let's now examine your relationship with yourself, your health-care relationships, your relationship with your spouse/partner, and your relationships with friends and family (the most important people in your life), and then let's focus on your top-twenty business list:

- **Relationship with yourself**—*You Go First.* You need to work on self-love and your mental fitness and have mastery in your relationship with yourself (for example, quieting the judge we met in the last chapter and thus achieving better mental health and self-confidence). If you love yourself, you will make self-care your number one priority (most CEOs don't do this, and there are serious consequences). If you are beating yourself up every day instead of celebrating your success every day, you won't have a lot of love to share with others. If you are not taking care of your health, including your mental health, this will lead to bad decisions and significant stress, anxiety, and serious health challenges. So many CEOs want to quit or sell their businesses because they stop believing in themselves and start questioning whether or not they are the right CEO for the business. It's heartbreaking for me when I think of CEOs I have known and worked with over the last twenty years who wanted to quit or sell because they were not making self-care their number one priority. In the US,

2024 had an 8.6 percent CEO turnover rate increase over the previous year.[22] Globally, CEO tenure has decreased from 8.1 years in Q1 of 2024 to a mere 6.8 years in Q1 of 2025.[23]

So many CEOs are no longer with us because they did not prioritize taking care of their health. According to *CEO Magazine*, 60 percent of CEO deaths are attributed to heart attacks.[24] I love my life, and self-care is my number one priority. I have a lot more love to give to my top-twenty business list and the people around me because I make self-care, self-love, and my mental health my number one priority—I remind myself and others that dead CEOs don't meet their targets on a regular basis. I usually get a chuckle when I say this because it really resonates with CEOs who are not taking care of their health. In our chapter on proactive health mastery, I discuss my sleep and health habits and the ones I recommend for CEOs.

I also use the 80/20 rule in all aspects of my life so I can enjoy the journey of life but be disciplined when I need to be. For example, when I'm on vacation, I drink more than the maximum two to four drinks a week that is recommended by my doctors, I don't eat 130 grams of protein every day, and I might not even work out every day if we are having late nights or when the hotels we are staying at don't have gyms.

---

22 Leslie Josephs, "From Nike to Intel, CEO Departures at U.S. Companies Hit a Record This Year," *CNBC*, December 20, 2024, https://www.cnbc.com/2024/12/20/ceo-departures-record-2024.html.

23 "Global CEO Turnover Index," Russell Reynolds, accessed June 5, 2025, https://www.russellreynolds.com/en/insights/reports-surveys/global-ceo-turnover-index.

24 Ramona Fasula, "CEOs and Heart Disease," *The CEO Magazine*, February 18, 2013, https://the-ceo-magazine.com/ceos-and-heart-disease/.

I don't beat myself up. I celebrate my 80/20 rule of enjoying the journey of life and living a healthy life most of the time.

However, I rarely sacrifice seven to eight hours of sleep each night because I know that it's very difficult to be my best self when I'm sleep-deprived. Over the past twenty years, I've learned that sleep deprivation is a pandemic at the top and that so many CEOs are sacrificing their health and mental fitness because they don't get enough sleep.

The other part of this relationship with yourself is mental toughness and how you inspire yourself every day and perform under pressure. A key aspect of successful relationship mastery involves showing up as the best version of yourself every day—even on the tough days. This means being a very caring, vulnerable, assertive human being (the CVA approach). Starting with self-love matters more than anything else. Loving yourself means doing things such as patting yourself on the back and not getting frustrated with yourself. It's about loving yourself even when other people don't show you the love. Using a 5:1 ratio of positivity to negativity with your own self-talk is a very high-impact strategy to give you greater access to your positive inspired brain every day.

Recognizing and eliminating stressful thoughts is also part of this self-relationship, understanding that your thoughts and feelings are not the truth. For example, you might be critical of yourself when you make a mistake and beat yourself up for an extended period of time. A better approach is to accept that you made a mistake (we are all human and make mistakes), apologize for your mistake by parking your ego/judge, and treat the mistake as a learning opportunity to help you show up as a better version of yourself in the future.

For me, as we discussed in the emotional mastery chapter, I try to show up 80 percent of the time as the very best version of myself in a positive emotional state (because it is not possible in life to be at 100 percent for 100 percent of the time; even thinking otherwise can cause burnout or extreme perfectionism). In my experience, most people have not done the hard work of mastering the ten MacKay Mastery areas of inspired leadership—and that's why they will show up only 20 percent of the time as their best self. The other 80 percent of the time they show up in a negative emotional state, for example, angry, annoyed, frustrated, hyper-critical, or difficult. To protect my personal relationship (me!), I "put on my Teflon shield" and do not allow someone else's negative emotions to penetrate my shield.

Instead, I have empathy and compassion for someone who shows up in a negative emotional state and do my very best to acknowledge their situation and get them into a positive emotional state. I ask them three powerful questions: What does success look like? What do you really want? If you knew you couldn't fail, what would you do? This gets people out of their fear/negative brain and into their inspired/positive brain so we can move forward in a positive direction. Our role as CEOs is to help the people around us get into a positive emotional state so they can show up as the best versions of themselves 80 percent of the time.

- **Healthcare relationships** include your family doctor and other healthcare professionals who will help you maximize your performance by ensuring that you are a healthy CEO. I have a family doctor, who is also my preventative executive health doctor, and I meet with her once a year to do a three-hour health assessment. I have a functional health/longevity doctor to help me achieve my goal of having a healthy lifespan until I get to 120 and go boom (I'm turning sixty this year, so I'm halfway there). I work with a virtual personal trainer three times a week on weight training, a virtual Pilates instructor once a week, a Zumba instructor once a weekend, and a Peloton instructor five times a week. I play squash with my twenty-six-year-old son once a week (he beats me really badly every game, so I literally have to practice mental fitness and parking my ego during each game). Having long-term relationships with people who help me take care of my health is a top priority for me.
- **Family and friend relationships** include your spouse/partner, kids, parents, friends, the people who are most important to you. My husband and kids are more important to me than anyone else, and having great long-term relationships with them is the second top priority in my life (self-care is my top priority, so I can show up as my best self with my family and friends). Unfortunately, CEOs have a higher-than-average divorce rate, often resulting in difficult relationships with their kids. I meet CEOs who missed out on countless events in their families' lives by prioritizing work and now they realize their children are practically strangers to them, or whose spouses are threatening to leave them—or have already done so. Prioritizing and mastering this area is essential to avoid deep regrets about

where and how you spent your time and attention. Spending time with and surrounding yourself with people you love and who love you is a critical mental health and confidence-building strategy for CEOs. When the going gets tough, I coach CEOs to help them reflect on what really matters most to them and remind them that they can handle anything and be unstoppable with a loving family supporting them.

- **Top-twenty business relationships** include your board, your top team, your business partners, your peers in your industry and outside your industry, external coaches/consultants, your customers, your suppliers, and your volunteer boards. At MacKay CEO Forums, we work with CEOs to help them identify and build relationships with game changers to help them achieve greater success in all areas of their lives. Most CEOs don't have a mindset of looking for game changers and asking for help, so they don't have a list of game changers to help them with their business, family, and personal goals. We live in an AI-enabled, exponential-change world, and game changers are so critical to CEO success.

You want to be intentional about having game changers on your board, on your top team, as external advisors, etc. Sometimes you have to pay for game changers; sometimes they are free (friends/family). The key is to have a mindset of finding game changers to help you achieve all of your goals.

For example, in the chapter about You Go First, I talked about a game changer for a CEO who wanted to expand in Europe and how valuable it was for him to meet a CEO who had taken that path before and achieved remarkable success by becoming the dominant player in his industry.

The CEO was thus able to save a lot of time by learning from the mistakes and successes of the new game changer in his life, and he had greater confidence and courage to set a big goal of becoming the dominant player in Europe in his industry because he got access to the game changer's proven road map to success.

Another CEO was struggling with teenage kids. I introduced him to my parenting coach, who worked with our family when our kids were teenagers. Although it was a bumpy ride, this parenting coach was a game changer and gave us new parenting skills, and we have great relationships with our kids now that they are in their twenties. This CEO's wife wanted him to quit his job or get a divorce because she was tired of being married to someone who was married to his job. I introduced him to Harville Hendrix's wisdom, including the book *Getting the Love You Want*,[25] as a game changer for his marriage. I can honestly say that Rob and I wouldn't be celebrating our twenty-seven-year elopement anniversary if it wasn't for relationship mastery game changers such as Harville Hendrix, John Gottman, and Gary Chapman, to name a few. I often meet CEOs who have contentious relationships with their boards and/or business partners. I've also seen my share of CEOs who have forgotten (or maybe never developed) the best ways to handle stress and who fly off the handle, resulting in failed partnerships, unhappy teams, and dissatisfied boards. Inspired leaders know that business is about people.

25 Harville Hendrix and Helen LaKelly Hunt, *Getting the Love You Want: A Guide for Couples*, 3rd ed. (St. Martin's Griffin, 2019).

By concentrating on relationship mastery, you strategically build and deepen the relationships that truly matter in your business, personal, and family lives, ensuring that it doesn't have to be lonely at the top. Inspired leaders are skilled at connecting, nurturing, and leveraging these relationships and understand that mastery in this area is fundamental to inspired leadership and overall success.

Strategic Relationship Mapping: Visualizing Your Connection Ecosystem

Relationship mastery, therefore, isn't just about being good with people in a general sense (though emotional intelligence and people skills are important). It's about applying strategic thinking to your network, both professional and personal, to ensure you have the support, challenge, and inspiration you need to succeed and thrive in all areas of life. Too often in the pursuit of success, it can be easy to lose sight of what matters and relationship priorities.

Building relationship mastery involves several key steps and habits. First, it's important to map your current relationship ecosystem. This means looking at all the key relationships in your life across business, personal, and family domains.

The next step is to identify relationship gaps. Where are you lacking support? Where are relationships not as strong as they need to be? This self-assessment helps you see where to focus your energy. Here are some key questions you could ask yourself:

Business: Am I building trust or relying only on authority? Who are the key people in my professional ecosystem, and how do I improve those relationships and build on them? Who in my current professional network could be a game changer for me?

Personal: Do I consistently make time for people who matter to me, or do I do so only when it's convenient? Am I truly present when I spend time with others, or am I distracted by work and devices? Do I surround myself with people who challenge and inspire me or only those who affirm me?

Family: Am I as intentional with my family as I am with my business? Do I schedule family time with the same urgency and non-negotiability as meetings? Am I modeling the kind of life and values I hope my family will embrace?

Next, you will want to be strategic and intentional about creating your top-twenty success team.

Building Your Top-Twenty Business Success Team

Having mapped your relationship ecosystem and identified key gaps, your next step is to intentionally identify and build your top-twenty business success team. This focused group of strategic relationships and game changers represents your most critical business connections, requiring deliberate selection and investment to address gaps and accelerate your leadership effectiveness.

Nurturing these relationships involves intentionality. When meeting new people, for instance, a high-impact strategy is to lead with generosity, asking, "How can I help you?" It's about cultivating a mindset of looking for game changers for any goal you set, whether business, family, or personal. Failing to surround yourself with game changers can leave you feeling isolated and is a big mistake that can lead to stress, anxiety, and relationships falling apart.

For a CEO, it doesn't have to be lonely at the top if you have a business success team of game changers that you love. This typically includes board members and/or business partners (and very importantly, your board chair), your top team, external mentors and advisors, and peer group connections. That last one is a key component (one I am passionate about—so passionate that I wrote this book), especially in today's world of exponential change. Many CEOs, even today, don't realize that peer support exists or how powerful it can be. Private companies often lack advisory boards, which I believe makes it almost impossible to win in today's environment.

External confidential peer support, in particular, is an area in which many CEOs have a gap, and it's essential for navigating today's AI-enabled, exponential-change world. CEOs have the same issues and challenges, so they can save a lot of time by learning from other CEO mistakes and lessons learned. CEOs can talk about everything—business, family, personal—with their peers, and their fellow CEOs can help them solve their toughest problems and maximize their best opportunities. We have found the most effective peer groups have twelve to sixteen members from diverse industries and backgrounds (no direct competitors). They are safe places to be vulnerable and tell the truth about what's really keeping you awake at night, with no competitors in the room.

Chairing my first peer group meeting twenty years ago was a huge aha moment for me, as I saw clearly how lonely it was at the top for these incredibly successful CEOs. Without a peer group, it's difficult for CEOs to find the right people to talk to about their challenges and opportunities. They can't talk to their board members about all of their business, family, and personal challenges (given their boards are responsible for hiring/firing the CEO). They can't talk to their top teams about certain confidential matters. Spouses/partners are not always in a position to offer the best support to CEOs. I remember telling my husband after I chaired my very first peer group meeting that this was what I was going to do for the rest of my life. I wanted to make sure that it wasn't going to be lonely at the top for the CEOs whom I was working with. I could also see that peer influence was far more impactful than any one-to-one CEO coaching work that I had ever done with CEOs. CEOs listen to each other and take action a lot quicker when they hear real stories of what worked or didn't work for others. CEO peer learning is the least time-intensive and the highest-impact approach to accelerating CEO performance (which is a lifelong journey).

The structure of these groups centers around approximately fourteen CEOs sitting around a boardroom table. A key element in forming these groups is ensuring they are diverse. This isn't about putting people who are all alike together. Instead, we seek diversity in areas such as ethnicity, gender, career stage, and industry. The aim is to surround members with people who offer different perspectives and points of view. This fosters a culture of innovation every meeting, every time, as CEOs are able to "steal" ideas from other industries and apply new ideas in their company. This is how they become industry leaders and transformers.

What these diverse peers all have in common is crucial: They are running successful businesses; they are learners, specifically lifelong learners; they genuinely want to contribute to the success of others (which is, after all, the very nature of peer support); and they are people who take action and want to raise their game and be the best versions of themselves in all areas of their lives.

The purpose of bringing these individuals together in a confidential setting is peer learning and mutual support. Because there are no competitors in the room, they can talk openly about everything—business, family, and personal matters. Their collective wisdom helps them solve their toughest problems and maximize their biggest opportunities. It provides them with crucial support and accountability, helps them save time, and offers a team of people to help them navigate life's challenges. Being around peers who are passionate about their work and lives can be contagious, fostering greater courage and confidence and reinforcing that they are not alone.

Daily Success Habits for Relationship Mastery

Building mastery in any area requires consistent practice, and relationships are no different. Yes, you can develop success habits for relationships just as you can for every mastery element we address. Here are some daily success habits for cultivating strong connections.

HABIT #1: MAINTAINING A 5:1 POSITIVITY TO NEGATIVITY RATIO IN INTERACTIONS

Habit 1 starts with the important tip to never criticize or say anything negative about yourself and/or another human being. Your ego/judge will say negative things about you, and about the people around you. You Go First means you never say anything negative about yourself. And when you do catch your judge, celebrate catching yourself and let it go. If you make a mistake, you accept it and move on or you stop to reflect on what the gift/learning is so you can avoid making the same mistake in the future. When you say something negative about another person, you catch your judge, celebrate that, and let it go. If another person makes a mistake, you accept it with empathy and compassion and show them love. When you say negative things about other people, you bust the trust in all relationships, so once you learn to stop complaining and making negative statements, you will have a lot more love to give yourself and others around you.

And, you'll be able to park your ego and apologize for your negative behaviors. Once you've mastered the first tip, positive relationships are about maintaining a ratio of 5:1 positivity to negativity, which is based on the research of Dr. John Gottman. He basically stated that we should have five positive encounters for every negative one.[26] This concept suggests that in relationships (especially challenging ones) it's important to have significantly more positive interactions or comments than negative ones. It's a very powerful tool in the tool kit to nurture business, family, and personal relationships.

One essential way to use this tool, especially for CEOs (and everyone else, frankly), is to catch people doing things right (including yourself) at least five times a day. You Go First means catching yourself doing things right all day long, thus building your self-confidence and self-love so you have more love to give others. For example, you could celebrate that you worked out, you were kind to your EA, you chose a healthy lunch, you closed a big deal—give yourself a pat on the back a minimum of five times a day to quiet the judge and you won't need anyone else to recognize you and cheer you on. When they do, it will be a bonus. When you catch other people doing things right at least five times a day and make a conscious effort to thank them or recognize them for how they showed up with a customer or board member, they feel the love—they feel heard, acknowledged, and appreciated. This builds a positive emotional bank account so that when you do need to have a more difficult conversation, you can do so within a context of overall positivity. Applying the 5:1 ratio to yourself, showing self-love and catching yourself doing things right, builds a positive personal emotional bank account and helps you

---

26 John M. Gottman and Robert W. Levenson, "Marital Processes Predictive of Later Dissolution: Behavior, Physiology, and Health," *Journal of Personality and Social Psychology 63, no. 2* (1992): 221-233, https://doi.org/10.1037/0022-3514.63.2.221.

maintain a positive emotional state 80 percent of the time regardless of others' actions.

HABIT #2: SENDING LOVE AND POSITIVE ENERGY TO PEOPLE AROUND YOU

This habit might sound unconventional in a business context. Not too many CEOs discuss the idea of business love in the workplace. However, my philosophy is grounded in the belief that every human being is an amazing human being. My goal every day is to show up as a CVA human being, the absolute best version of myself. And in that mindset, I approach people from a place of love. I don't necessarily love all of their behaviors, but I love them as human beings. Love is the most important basic human need. I discovered the power of tools such as the five love languages (see box), initially applying it to my husband and kids and then bringing it into my work with CEOs. It's a game-changing tool that helps you understand how others receive love and appreciation, whether it's through verbal appreciation, gifts (something as simple as a gift card that shows appreciation can be so meaningful for some people), quality time, or other forms. These gestures can be incredibly powerful.

HABIT #3: DAILY RELATIONSHIP-NURTURING PRACTICES

If you want to achieve relationship mastery in order to have positive, fulfilling long-term relationships in all areas of your life, you will need to be strategic about how you spend your time and whom you spend it with.

Building new relationships and deepening existing relationships daily can take various forms:

Sending love and positive energy to people around you. This success habit starts by seeing every human being as amazing and focusing on their strengths versus their weaknesses. See their mistakes or behaviors as separate from who they are as an amazing human being.

Showing up as a CVA human being. Practicing CVA on a daily basis is often life-changing for people's relationships. The best part is you can use the CVA tool kit to deepen all of your business, family, and personal relationships.

Using self-love practices. These include avoiding beating yourself up and recognizing that self-judgment comes from the judge, or fear brain. The two valid options when you notice the judge are to accept it or learn from it. In addition, use positive self-messaging. This involves using a daily mantra such as "I'm enough; I'm a gem; I'm a beautiful person; I'm a lovable person" to get grounded, especially when judging yourself. Gratitude journaling, practiced nightly, involves reflecting on what you are grateful for, thus filling your head with gratitude, which is the opposite of stress and anxiety. Gratitude is an emotion you can practice accessing all day long. Finally, self-love involves taking care of your physical and mental health. For me, this includes daily positive intelligence breathing, sufficient sleep (seven to eight hours daily), daily exercise, and healthy eating. It is impossible to achieve a positive emotional state without these basics.

DEEPER DIVE: THE FIVE LOVE LANGUAGES

Observing and being aware of these love languages and how they impact our relationships can be a game changer. I know that using the word *love* in the business world takes some getting used to for many CEOs. I think one important game changer for me was learning about the five love languages. Introduced by author Dr. Gary Chapman, these concepts apply to business, family, and personal relationships.[27]

Words of affirmation: This is catching people doing things right using our 5:1 ratio and letting them know.

Acts of service: This language is doing helpful things for your business relationships, such as getting others set up for success and always finding ways to help them be successful with their goals.

Receiving gifts: For some, receiving gifts that tell them you were thinking about them and appreciate them is their love language. A small gift card or thank-you card, or tickets to see their favorite sports team, are simple gestures that can mean much for the recipient.

Quality time: This is spending meaningful time with business relationships (put away your phones!). It could be having breakfast or coffee, lunch, or dinner to talk about all aspects of their lives—not just business.

Physical touch: This love language involves shaking hands, giving someone a high five or pat on the back, or hugs in the workplace to create a culture of love.

One thing to note, from a spouse/partner perspective, is that we all have a love language we tend to use—and one we would appreciate in return. These do not always match. So, for example, a husband who cleaned the kitchen after

27 Gary Chapman, *The 5 Love Languages: The Secret to Love That Lasts* (Northfield Publishing, 2024).

dinner might feel as if that was an act of love—but his spouse might be someone who appreciates quality time. This same principle holds for business relationships. If you use a personalized approach to show business love, you will build a closer connection with your business relationships. For some people, quality time really matters. For others, a thank-you card means everything.

CEO Success Story

Relationship mastery has a profound impact, not just on personal well-being but on business outcomes and long-term success. One story that comes to mind highlights this vividly, echoing the biggest time-mastery mistake that CEOs make. We saw it in the time-mastery chapters—the 24/7 trap.

I was having dinner with a CEO who was about to turn fifty. He was celebrating a milestone birthday, ten years leading his company, and a significant anticipated payout. By all external measures, he was incredibly successful. But despite this professional achievement, he was questioning everything. He felt like his whole life was a wreck outside of his CEO role. He was even considering quitting his job because he had enough money and felt the need to find something else to do with his life, implying that the relentless 24/7 trap had cost him dearly in other areas.

This CEO was a classic example of someone who had sacrificed personal and family relationships at the expense of business success. He had allowed the demands of the job to consume his life, leaving little room for the relationships that truly nourish and sustain us.

We worked together to address this. I encouraged him to believe that his success wasn't *because* he worked 24/7, and that he could be incredibly successful while also having a fulfilling life outside of work. This involved helping him figure out how to master his time (another of our MacKay Mastery Model areas) and set boundaries. We went through the process of defining what success looked like for him in all areas, not just business. What did success look like with his marriage? With his kids? With his health? This exercise revealed a strong desire to continue being a successful CEO *and* have a great marriage, time for his kids, and time for his health.

We focused on powerful questions such as What does success look like? What do you really want? and What makes you jump out of bed every morning with passion? These questions helped him identify his purpose, something he initially struggled with. His purpose ultimately revolved around making a difference in other people's lives, extending beyond just his company.

Using tools such as the one-hundred-hour week tool kit (which helps analyze how time is spent) and the Unstoppable CEO ninety-day plan tool kit (available on our website), he was able to regain control over his life. He learned to be intentional about how he spent his time and who he spent it with. Fast-forward to today, he is still running the company and is living the dream—not sacrificing his health, marriage, and relationships with his friends and family.

This story demonstrates that prioritizing and nurturing relationships is not a distraction from business success but an *integral part* of sustainable, inspired leadership. It shows that mastering relationships can directly impact a CEO's well-being, their ability to lead effectively, and their long-term fulfillment.

Deeper Dive: Harville Hendrix

One of my game changers is Harville Hendrix. He wrote the book *Getting the Love You Want: A Guide for Couples*, which has sold millions of copies and exponentially changed many people's lives.[28] While the seven principles I share here are geared toward couples, you can see that, fundamentally, they are brilliant rules for You Go First and for reflecting on what you can do to be the best spouse/partner you can be and showing up as the best version of yourself in your love relationship. These exact same principles apply to business relationships such as those with business partners, people on your top team, and board members. He advises taking the following actions:

- Discover why you choose your partner.
- Resolve the power struggle that prevents greater intimacy.
- Learn to listen to your partner.
- Begin healing early childhood experiences.
- Become passionate friends with your partner.
- Achieve a shared vision of your dream relationship.[29]

In addition to identifying your spouse, friends, and family members as game changers, it can be tempting to think of business game changers as only those people with whom you have business relationships. However, your game changers can also be the brilliant thought leaders who choose to share their wisdom through books, podcasts, or learning events. If, as you read this chapter, you realized your relationships are suffering,

28 Harville Hendrix, *Getting the Love You Want: A Guide for Couples* (Henry Holt and Company, 1988).

29 Elizabeth Hedges, "Dr Harville Hendrix and the Art of Conscious Relationships," *Offspring Magazine*, August 25, 2020, https://offspringmagazine.com.au/wellspring/dr-harville-hendrix-and-the-art-of-conscious-relationships/.

you may wish to refer to thought leaders who have achieved relationship mastery (e.g., Hendrix, Gottman, Chapman). Their road maps to success are readily available through books, podcasts, etc.

END-OF-CHAPTER CHECK-IN

Rate the following on a Likert scale (e.g., 1 = strongly disagree, 5 = strongly agree), and get your score:

RELATIONSHIP MASTERY

- I consistently nurture trusted relationships in all areas of my life.
- I express appreciation, love, and honesty in professional and personal interactions.
- I consciously build and maintain my top-twenty business list.

RELATIONSHIP MASTERY REFLECTION

Who on my top-twenty business list haven't I thanked, appreciated, or connected with recently?

GAME CHANGER PROMPT

Who models meaningful connection and trust? Who helps me build and strengthen relationships across my life?

CHAPTER 7
PASSION MASTERY

Passion will move men beyond themselves, beyond their shortcomings, beyond their failures.
—JOSEPH CAMPBELL

When I realized I could have a greater impact by working with CEOs, and that I had a real, actionable plan to end the kind of loneliness experienced by those at the top, I knew I had found my passion. I came home from chairing my first peer group meeting, and I knew that this was what I was *meant* to do. I literally told my husband that this was what I wanted to do for the rest of my life. That type of passion is what sustains us through struggles and challenges.

In this chapter, we turn our attention to a vital component of leading an inspired life and inspiring others: passion mastery.

This chapter is about discovering and harnessing the power of your inner drive. According to our framework, passion mastery is about identifying your strengths, understanding your purpose, and clearly defining your *why*. Why do you jump out of bed in the morning, feeling like you just can't wait to start your day? It's about leveraging this deep self-knowledge so you can show up each day ready to make the biggest contribution in all areas of your life. (Conversely, if you have lost your *why*, hopefully this chapter can help ignite it again.)

As with all ten areas of the MacKay Mastery Model, passion mastery is a lifelong journey. I review on a quarterly basis my level of passion for all areas of my wheel of life, and I identify the areas that need more work. I use the same approach when I'm coaching CEOs on their ninety-day plans. I remember coaching a founder CEO who had recently sold his business for hundreds of millions of dollars and successfully transitioned out of the business. He had achieved his goal of financial freedom at the age of fifty-five. He showed up for his ninety-day coaching session with me, and he said he had never been so depressed in his entire life. He said he had made a big mistake by selling his business because he had no passion to jump out of bed in the morning and his wife was getting frustrated with him hanging around the house and getting in her way.

I asked, "What would make you jump out of bed in the morning with the same amount of passion and energy that you had before you sold your business?" He said, "If I let my one-year noncompete run out and started a new business in the same industry, I would be able to get my passion and energy back and build an even bigger and better business. I could probably attract a lot of the top talent from my former company if they are not happy with their new owner."

That's exactly what he did, and he went back to living the dream as a successful entrepreneur! I often say to CEOs that purpose-driven motivation sustains leaders through challenges. If you live your life with passion, you will be able to overcome all challenges and be unstoppable in all aspects of your life.

I believe that passion enables us to show up as inspired human beings in all aspects of our lives. For example, a few years ago, my husband and I bought a place in Scottsdale, Arizona, and as new snowbirds we didn't know anyone in our community. Our plan was to live in Scottsdale for five to six months each year and in Vancouver for five to six months each year. For the first year, I felt lonely and sad and wondered if we had made the right decision. I realized that I needed to work on building new friendships as a critical passion mastery strategy. I found a game changer who runs the social committee in our community, and I signed Rob and I up for monthly wine tastings to get to know people in our community. For six months of that first year, it took a lot of energy to build new friendships. However, the six months of the second year were a blast with our Scottsdale friends and lots of Canadian friends visiting us. I also signed up for Zumba classes in Scottsdale and rediscovered my passion for dancing. Now, I enjoy dancing once a week with my Zumba friends in Scottsdale (and in Vancouver). And, of course, I have a Zumba instructor in Scottsdale who is my game changer and gives me greater confidence and courage to learn how to do Zumba (and quiet my judge as I stand at the back of the room and make the inevitable rookie mistakes).

Think about success in the context of passion mastery. It means having absolute clarity on what your purpose is. It means being passionate about that purpose, right down to the specific activities that bring it to life. When you achieve passion mastery, you're able to be intentional about how you spend your time across all areas of your life—your business, your family, and your personal life. Finding game changers to help you continue to be passionate about all areas of your life is key. You know where to direct your energy because you're guided by your deepest values and your clearest *why*. It's about living that purpose every single day in everything you do. As the great philosopher Friedrich Nietzsche famously wrote, "He who has a why to live can bear almost any how."[30]

At MacKay CEO Forums, our dream is to populate the world with inspiring leaders. This isn't just a slogan; it's the driving force behind everything we do. And that dream starts with me, as the founder and CEO. I have to go first. I have to ask myself every day, "Am I living that purpose? Am I achieving that purpose in all that I do?" This personal commitment is the foundation of passion mastery.

I've had many CEOs ask me, "How did you find your purpose?" and "Can you have more than one purpose?"

My answer is *yes* to having more than one purpose. Whatever helps you jump out of bed in the morning feeling like you just can't wait to get started making a huge contribution in all areas of your life is your purpose. If you have more than one purpose, then that's great!

My answer to how I found my purpose goes back to 2005, when I decided to quit my job as a professor to become an entrepreneur. I started thinking deeply about that question. What drives consistent motivation and energy? And I came up with my first purpose statement: I want to help other people be successful and achieve their full potential. From a You Go First perspective, I wanted to learn how to achieve my full potential so I could make the biggest contribution in all areas of my life. My purpose statement evolved when I started chairing CEO peer groups and saw that it was lonely at the top for CEOs because they didn't have peers to help them solve their toughest problems and maximize their best opportunities. It's very difficult for CEOs to show up as inspiring leaders without peer support. CEOs who have fourteen peers (and their forum chair) who believe in them and are there for them throughout the bumpy ride of business and life

30 Friedrich Nietzsche, *Twilight of the Idols: or How to Philosophize with a Hammer*, trans. Duncan Large, Oxford World's Classics (Oxford University Press, 2008).

are far more likely to show up as inspiring leaders. I came up with my *big dream* (and we all should have big dreams) of populating the world with inspiring leaders so that CEOs and the people around them can show up as inspiring leaders and achieve their full potential. This same dream/purpose holds true for everyone in my life, including friends, family, volunteers, etc.

If you feel stuck by the question of finding or articulating your purpose, there are even AI-enabled approaches to finding your purpose in today's world. An AI bot asks you a bunch of questions and then comes up with a draft purpose statement. I used one of these tools to validate my purpose and to help my husband and kids find their purposes. I've also used this tool with one of my CEO groups that I chair and with my top team to help them find purpose statements.

Success in passion mastery begins with a clear personal understanding of your purpose, which is often described as an overarching dream or mission (such as populating the world with inspiring leaders!). This purpose energizes you in the morning and makes you feel really good about how you're spending your days, not just at work but also in your volunteer work, with your kids, and in all aspects of your life. I've shared, for example, how taking care of my health is nonnegotiable. It is a lot easier to wake up at four in the morning and hit the Peloton when I know it's to keep me in peak performance so I can continue to share my passion with the world.

To achieve success, it's important to identify the activities that give you positive energy and that you love to do. Using tools such as StrengthsFinder 2.0 can be powerful in this process, as oftentimes, when you're doing activities that are in your areas of strength, you become a lot more passionate about what you're doing (see box). At MacKay CEO Forums, we often use this tool during our annual CEO retreats. All fourteen CEOs attend the retreat and use the

StrengthsFinder 2.0 tool in advance. We have every CEO share their top-five strengths, and they set their ninety-day plan to build on their strengths. We ask them to identify their top-three business, family, and personal goals for the quarter and to step into their strengths as they determine their areas of focus. If they have goals that are not aligned with their strengths, we challenge them to find other people on their top team to take on those goals so they can free up their time to focus on the goals that are aligned with their strengths. We use this same principle for business, family, and personal goals. CEOs leave the retreat inspired to share the StrengthsFinder 2.0 passion mastery team-building exercise with their top teams to take their passion to the next level.

STRENGTHSFINDER 2.0

The StrengthsFinder 2.0 tool (developed by Gallup, Inc.; now CliftonStrengths) is an incredibly popular assessment, developed by Don Clifton while he was leading the polling company. Test-takers are given paired statements, and they pick the statement that they most relate to. The results show the test-takers their top-five areas of strength.

My personal top-five strengths are: achiever, relator, learner, winning others over, and self-assurance. I've spent many years working on building on these strengths and ensuring that I use all of them to make the biggest contribution in all areas of my life. I rely on my board, top team, and external resources with other strengths to take on roles that are aligned with their strengths. We spend time catching each other doing things right and ensuring that everyone is focused on building their strengths.

StrengthsFinder 2.0 has four primary strength domains: strategic thinking, relationship building, influencing, and executing. But within each of those domains are additional strengths (thirty-four in total).

- **Strategic thinking:** analytical, context, futuristic, ideation, input, intellection, learner, strategic
- **Relationship building:** adaptability, connectedness, developer, empathy, harmony, includer, individualization, positivity, relator
- **Influencing:** activator, command, communication, competition, maximizer, self-assurance, significance, woo
- **Executing:** achiever, arranger, belief, consistency, deliberative, discipline, focus, responsibility, restorative[31]

Knowing our strengths allows us to build on them and see our positive attributes. (This tool is also a great one for leaders trying to understand their teams.)

Another key aspect of defining success in passion mastery is aligning actions with values. This alignment interrelates with your purpose and passion. Your purpose statement, for instance, can be the same as your company's dream, especially if you are the founder. Aligning your personal values with your actions is important.

---

31 "The 34 CliftonStrengths Themes Explain Your Talent DNA," CliftonStrengths, https://www.gallup.com/cliftonstrengths/en/253715/34-cliftonstrengths-themes.aspx.

Passion is about your intrinsic motivation (what's inside, inspiring you) not extrinsic motivation (such as getting a promotion or recognition from others).

Discovering Your Purpose Leads to Passion

When you have a clear purpose, you feel good about how you are spending your days across all aspects of your life, including work, volunteer activities, and time with your family (and time by yourself as well).

Discovering your purpose can be a journey. StrengthsFinder 2.0 or other tools can be one method of discovery. Keeping a "passion journal" by tracking activities you love doing versus those you don't can be another discovery tool to help align your time with your areas of strength and passion. For example, I challenged myself to do a passion journal for a seven-day period to take a deeper dive on the activities I do on a daily basis. I rated each activity on a scale of 1 to 5 (low to high). I delegated, outsourced, or stopped doing everything that I rated 1 to 3. I do this on a quarterly basis, so I'm always staying passionate about being the CEO of MacKay CEO Forums. And, I'm creating the space to innovate and allow others to step up and take on roles that they are passionate about.

On an annual basis, I fire myself as the CEO of MacKay CEO Forums (I do this on January 1 each year, and I've been doing this for about ten years). I step one year into the future, and I ask myself, "What are all of the accomplishments that I'm celebrating (business, family, personal)?" I then complete my Q1 ninety-day plan on the first day of my job as the new CEO of MacKay CEO Forums. This exercise really helps me stay passionate about my CEO role and let go of the past year in order to free up new energy for the coming year. I share this with my top team, and I ask them to do the same celebration exercise to help them stay passionate about their roles. We have a sample 2026 Celebration tool that we rolled out across all of our forum chairs/members this year.

When I coach others on creating a purpose statement, I try to keep it simple, as people can overthink it and create statements they won't remember. We've all seen companies with mission statements no one can recall. A purpose statement requires you to live it—so you want to remember it.

A direct question I use to help uncover purpose is What makes you jump out of bed in the morning and do what you do? Initial responses might focus on success or making money, but I dig deeper: Imagine all that's happened. You have the success and the money, so what gives you pure joy? What's the fundamental reason why you jump out of bed in the morning?

Very often, with this exercise clients arrive at a simple statement such as "I want to build future leaders," "I want to make a difference for my employees," or "I want to pass along my wisdom to the next generation." Today, you can even use AI tools to ask questions that can help clarify purpose.

Having a purpose statement is important for several reasons. It aligns your actions with your values. It helps you stay positive and focused and can help you achieve your longer-term vision. Furthermore, when facing challenges or considering quitting, reminding yourself of your purpose helps you evaluate if stopping aligns with your fundamental reason for doing what you do. Without purpose, even finding something else to do might not lead to fulfillment or the energy to jump out of bed every day. That is why the CEO I told you about who was considering quitting needed to reconnect with his relationships and rediscover his passion. He was burned-out, but just quitting would not have solved the underlying issue.

Success in passion mastery isn't just about personal fulfillment; it also has a significant impact on leadership effectiveness and organizational performance. When leaders find this alignment of purpose and passion, it allows them to show up as inspired leaders, going first and inspiring themselves. This self-inspiration then enables them to inspire others.

Maintaining passion over the long haul, given that the leadership journey can be bumpy, is also part of success. Strategies for fostering and maintaining passion in business, family, and personal realms include surrounding yourself with people who are very passionate, positive, and purpose-led. Both negativity and passion are like viruses—they can spread. Choose who you want to be around. Surrounding yourself with people who live with passion and those aligned with your purpose is magic.

Identifying game changers—such as CEO coaches with a proven road map to success—is another effective strategy. Ensuring that they have extensive experience coaching CEOs is a key selection criteria if you are going to use this strategy.

Additionally, having your forum chair or an external CEO coach who can hold up a mirror and make you aware if you're not showing up as an inspired leader helps in maintaining passion mastery. Business is a bumpy ride—and that's when external advisors can remind us of our passion and purpose.

Ultimately, passion mastery allows you to live a life in which you spend most of your time on activities you love, contributing in meaningful ways and showing up as your best inspired self.

Your Daily Passion Boost

So, how do you begin to unlock this mastery? One of the most powerful tools I use, and one we discuss in our peer groups, involves asking yourself three simple questions on a daily basis. These three questions are a daily practice, a habit that anchors you in your purpose throughout the day as you prepare for important meetings, presentations, and conversations.

1. What does success look like?
2. What do you really want?
3. What is your purpose?

Asking these three questions regularly helps you stay in your positive inspired brain. You're not starting the day thinking of your problems but rather looking at what inspires you and why you are here. When you focus on what success looks like, what you truly want, and your underlying purpose, you shift your mindset. It's a powerful way to combat negativity and stay focused, whether you're interacting with others or spending time on your own.

I use these questions constantly. Before I attend a meeting, I mentally prepare by asking myself these questions to ensure I show up focused and ready to make the biggest impact possible. It helps me be present and show up as the best version of myself. It's not about ignoring challenges but about framing them from a place of purpose and desired outcome.

So, before a meeting, I will ask myself, "What would success for this meeting look like?" Then, "What do I want from this meeting?

What is my ideal outcome?" Finally, "What is my purpose here?" So, for example, if I am coaching someone, then my purpose is to help them achieve a positive outcome and mindset, a plan, and a goal.

This practice is fundamental because, as we discussed in chapter 1, we need to figure out how to inspire ourselves first. Asking these questions is a core strategy for doing just that. These three passion questions connect directly to living your purpose every day.

Applying these questions to each area of your life—business, family, and personal—is important. The questions are simple yet help you clarify your purpose and focus on what success looks like and what you really want, which is essential for maintaining inspired leadership, particularly during challenging times. If you know your purpose, you can always return to it instead of feeling like you need to quit when the journey is bumpy.

The Six Human Needs: Identifying Your Core Drivers

Author Tony Robbins has said that the human need for contribution is about wanting to make a difference in other people's lives. This can relate to family, friends, community, or even country. He has identified six basic human needs—including contribution (which I think of as part of purpose). The six needs are: certainty, uncertainty/variety, significance, connection/love, growth, and contribution.[32] Understanding which of the six basic human needs, particularly contribution, are most important to you can inform your purpose and passion. If you feel you aren't making a contribution, success in this area means figuring out *who* you want to impact and *how*.

32 "Discover the 6 Human Needs," Tony Robbins, accessed May 1, 2025, https://www.tonyrobbins.com/blog/do-you-need-to-feel-significant.

Let's explore each of these needs:

1. **Certainty:** This is the need for safety, security, stability, comfort, and predictability. While some people need a lot more certainty than others, it matters to everyone to some degree. Recognizing how important certainty is to oneself, without judgment, is key. Remember, this is supposed to be a judgment-free leadership zone. Practical ways to create certainty can involve setting boundaries around things like your schedule. If certainty is one of your top needs, finding ways to feel you are in a safe space and creating habits that provide predictability can be helpful.
2. **Uncertainty/variety:** This need encompasses the desire for change, challenge, excitement, and surprise. It is seen as the opposite of certainty, addressing the human tendency to get bored with repetition. While some people are comfortable with routine, others strongly need variety. We all know serial entrepreneurs who get one company off the ground, sell it, and move on to the next start-up. Or people who change jobs every few years, seeking new challenges.
3. **Significance:** This is the need to feel important, unique, special, and needed. It relates to seeking recognition from others. A significant aspect of mastering this need involves learning how to create significance for yourself, so you do not depend on others to provide that recognition. It also involves surrounding oneself with people who won't judge you and will recognize and honor that significance matters to you.
4. **Connection/love:** Highlighted as the number one basic human need, this encompasses the need for connection, intimacy, and love. The concept of love in a business context

is described as being openhearted and caring enough about people to tell the truth. It's about bringing that judgment-free leadership into the workplace. Self-love is considered foundational to this—we cannot love others until we learn to love ourselves. Satisfying this need involves surrounding ourselves with people who love us and offer deep connection.

5. **Growth:** This book celebrates lifelong learning. This need is the intrinsic drive for continuous improvement, acquiring new skills, and personal development. People for whom this need is particularly strong are constantly striving for improvement and challenges.
6. **Contribution:** This need relates to making a difference in other people's lives, serving others, and contributing to something beyond oneself. For leaders, making a difference for CEOs has an exponential impact because of the multiplier effect, as they then help many people. This is one reason I founded MacKay CEO Forums. By providing peer support for so many CEOs, my contributions act as a force multiplier, and countless people benefit from healthy leadership. Contribution is often identified as a significant need, particularly later in one's career.

Understanding these needs ties back directly to the core principle of You Go First leadership. By becoming aware of and learning to satisfy our own basic human needs, we are better equipped to show up as our best selves. This self-mastery allows leaders to have more energy and love to give to the rest of the world.

Identifying your top two basic human needs from the six discussed can also be leveraged to develop your purpose statement. For example, if contribution is a top need, figuring out who and how to make a difference in other people's lives will help you create your purpose statement.

Daily Success Habits for Passion Mastery

The daily success habits for passion mastery aren't complex processes; they are simple, consistent practices that keep you connected to your purpose. Here are three that can make a difference.

HABIT #1: LIVE YOUR PURPOSE EVERY DAY

This is the overarching habit. It means consciously asking yourself throughout the day whether your actions align with your core purpose and mission. Am I showing up as an inspired leader? Am I making the difference I intend to make?

Use the three passion questions we discussed earlier—multiple times a day. Check in with yourself.

1. What is success?
2. What do you want?
3. What is your purpose?

Also, look at your work calendar, look at your family or personal calendar. Your calendars should reflect your purpose too. Rate your passions from 1 to 5 for your daily/weekly/monthly activities (1 is the lowest; 5 the highest). Get those 1-, 2-, and maybe even 3-level tasks and meetings off your calendar. Assign them to others who are passionate about those activities. Focus 80 percent of your time on activities that make you passionate each day. Be an exemplar for your top team so they are inspired to follow your lead.

HABIT #2: KEEP A PASSION JOURNAL

A practical approach mentioned briefly earlier is keeping a passion journal for a period. For two or three weeks, track activities you love and those you don't love (a deeper dive look at that calendar). This helps you figure out which activities could be delegated. Ideally, you want most of your time to be spent doing activities that are in your areas of strength and that you're very passionate about. This intentional focus on leveraging strengths and engaging in activities in your areas of strength are key to maximizing your passion on a daily basis.

HABIT #3: BUILD ON YOUR STRENGTHS, BUILD ON YOUR PASSIONS

Contrary to popular wisdom, it's far more efficient and impactful to focus your time and energy on your areas of strength and passion. In my two decades of experience in this area, I have seen that only a small percentage of CEOs and executives do what they do best every day. In fact, a minimum of 80 percent of your time should be spent in your areas of strength, and everything else should be delegated or outsourced.

These habits ensure that you will be able to deliver extraordinary results.

Here is a success formula that I use when I'm coaching CEOs:

Passion + competence + need = extraordinary results

Passion is more important than anything else in the success formula. If you have passion, you will find a way to build the competence you need to succeed. If you don't have passion, you will likely give up when the going gets tough.

Consciously seek opportunities throughout your day to apply your top strengths in your interactions and tasks. Using the StrengthsFinder 2.0 tool or self-observation (or meeting with mentors and accountability partners), consider your strengths—and build on them. For example, if "relator" is a strength, focus on deepening connections; if "achiever" is a strength, prioritize making progress on key tasks.

CEO Success Story

I was having dinner with a CEO, and he said to me, "We're going to celebrate three things. I'm turning fifty. I've been the CEO of this company for ten years. And I'm going to get a big payout at the end of this year. And so, if I wanted to, I could quit my job as a CEO and I could buy a winery, or I could take my kids out of school and go traveling around the world with my wife and family."

I suppose most of us have those lottery-like daydreams sometimes. But I wondered if those dreams of his would really be fulfilling.

I said, "You're this incredibly successful CEO. Why would you want to quit? You are incredibly talented."

He listed common reasons I hear—he'd been married to his job, his relationships were rocky because of that, and he just felt empty inside—despite the fact that we were supposed to be celebrating.

I started working with him on time mastery. But in a nutshell, it is a critical element of purpose, because when you know what your purpose is, you can be really clear about how you spend your time, whom you spend your time with, and so on.

We went through an exercise in which I asked him what success would look like.

He said, "Well, I guess I would continue to be a CEO, I'd have a great marriage, I'd have time for my kids, and I'd have time for my health."

Next I asked, "And what is it that you really want?"

Since he had worked with me a bit, he had a great answer: "I want to be able to show up as the best version of myself every day."

And then, when I said, "What's your purpose?" he drew a blank.

So we decided to do some deep exploration around what his purpose was, because when the going gets tough and you feel like quitting, if you remind yourself of what your purpose is, then you don't lose sight of the mission.

I said, "Let's really think about why you jump out of bed in the morning. You work really hard, and you put all this time in. So what drives that?"

That's when he said, "Well, to be honest with you, I really love building future leaders. I love really everything I can do to get my team set up for success and to learn and grow myself. But building future leaders and giving other people the opportunity that I've had to get to the top is what really excites me." I said, "OK, well, what if your purpose is building future leaders, and that could be your kids or people at work? It could be in your volunteer world. But that's what you're going to be focused on."

I told him to really step into that purpose every day, to reframe his thinking to *My purpose is that I'm making a difference, and that's meaningful to me.*

He held on to that, and practiced it, and it gave him a lot more alignment in his life around his purpose.

Identify Your Game Changers for Passion Mastery

As with any area of mastery, you don't have to figure it all out on your own. Passion mastery has its own set of game changers. These can be individuals you hire, such as a coach, or resources such as books and mentors.

In the realm of passion mastery, relevant game changers might include thought leaders who provide frameworks for identifying strengths, purpose, and motivation. Here are some powerful tools and resources:

- **StrengthsFinder 2.0:** A tool to help identify your natural talents.
- **Simon Sinek:** He wrote the books *Start with Why* and *Find Your Why*. I love this quote: "The goal is not simply for you to cross the finish line, but to see how many people you can inspire to run with you." And, important to our chapter, "If we want to feel an undying passion for our work, if we want to feel we are contributing to something bigger than ourselves, we all need to know our WHY."[33]
- **Tony Robbins:** Tony wrote the book *Unleash the Power Within* and developed a program with the same name. You may be familiar with him through his books, audiobooks, countless interviews, and events. His program focuses on human needs and motivation. Robbins promises to unleash the fire within. We all have one—but sometimes the flame starts to sputter out. This program helps awaken personal passion. You can read his books—or attend one of his events. Either way, tapping into your personal power is a game changer.

Engaging with these game changers can provide valuable insights and tools as you explore your own passion and purpose. Sometimes, you need many game changers to achieve your goals. The key is shifting

33 Simon Sinek, David Mead, and Peter Docker, *Find Your Why: A Practical Guide to Discovering Purpose for You and Your Team* (Penguin Books, 2017).

your mindset from needing to figure everything out yourself to actively seeking out those who already have proven road maps.

By identifying your purpose, needs, and *why*, you're setting the foundation for leadership that is truly meaningful and motivating. Mastering your passion isn't just about feeling good; it's about directing your incredible energy and talent toward making the biggest impact possible, starting with yourself and radiating outward. It's a cornerstone of inspired leadership.

Who are the people on your top-twenty list for the next ninety days? And critically, what's the difference you want to make with them? When you combine your understanding of your purpose and needs with the specific individuals you want to impact, you create a powerful road map for action.

Assessing the impact of aligned purpose on performance is part of this journey. When CEOs find this alignment between their personal purpose and their leadership role, they see a significant positive impact. Their passion becomes fuel for their performance and the performance of their organization.

END-OF-CHAPTER CHECK-IN

Rate the following on a Likert scale (e.g., 1 = strongly disagree, 5 = strongly agree), and get your score:

PASSION MASTERY

- I am clear on my purpose and recommit to it daily.
- I know what success looks like for me across personal and professional domains.
- I align my goals and calendar with what gives me energy and meaning.

PASSION MASTERY REFLECTION

What's one thing I could do tomorrow that aligns deeply with my *why* and brings me joy?

GAME CHANGER PROMPT

Who lives with purpose and passion? Who could help me reconnect with my strengths and clarify my *why*?

CHAPTER 8
INNOVATION MASTERY

Innovation is the ability to see change as opportunity—not a threat.
—STEVE JOBS

One of the most exciting things about working with CEOs is their natural affinity for innovation. They are often iconoclasts and innovators. This isn't just about coming up with a new idea. It's about always looking for new ideas, within your industry and outside of your industry, that could be applied to your business with game-changing results. This mastery area is about raising your game as a CEO so you can be an industry disrupter, transformer, and leader.

For example, four key sources of new ideas and innovation are

1. your company, customers, suppliers, partners, and key stakeholders;
2. your industry (getting involved with industry conferences/associations and sitting on boards);
3. other industries, through cross-industry peer support and sitting on boards (if you only spend time with CEOs in

your own industry, this will limit your ability to get access to potentially game-changing new ideas for your business); and

4. individual reflection and ideation time.

On that last one, most people mistakenly believe that innovation (taking a new idea and applying it to your business) can only truly happen when you're brainstorming in a room with others. However, my experience, and that of others, shows that many ideas actually spring from creating dedicated space for your inspired, creative, positive brain to operate. For example, Google famously allocates 20 percent of time for employees to work on their passion projects—and Gmail actually came out of this innovative approach.[34] When that inspired brain kicks in, we can generate new ideas, make truly great decisions, solve problems more effectively, and get into action. For example, I generate a lot of new ideas every morning during my twelve-minute guided PQ reps. I also generate a lot of new ideas while cycling daily on my Peloton, and when I'm on a West Vancouver seawall walk. We all have activities and places that inspire us. I write down all of my new ideas in my monthly planning journal so I can review the ideas on a daily, weekly, monthly, and quarterly basis. I'm always excited about my next ninety-day plan because I can apply new ideas and take action in all areas of my life to stay inspired and drive business results. I'm also a believer in failing fast—if I am not making progress on a new idea, then I let go and move on.

Innovation involves applying new ideas to create improved business, family, or personal outcomes, whether it's with your customers, your financials, your operations, or your technology—it doesn't matter what part of business; a new idea applied means you

---

34 Claire Anderson, "What Is Innovation Time Allocation?" *Focus Keeper*, October 1, 2024, https://focuskeeper.co/glossary/what-is-innovation-time-allocation.

get new results. It doesn't even have to be a new idea. It could be an idea applied to a new context. For example, with my family, during the COVID-19 pandemic, my son and daughter moved back home to finish university online. We had dinners together every night, and I had an idea that we could use a red, yellow, green tool to talk about our feelings and bring us closer together during very challenging times. This tool is often used to discuss business results, so I really wasn't sure if it would work with my family. At the first few dinners, there was a lot of eye-rolling from my husband and kids and a lot of reluctance and resistance. After a few dinners, I shared that I really wanted everyone to embrace this new tool so every dinner could be a fun family experience (FFE is a term we use in the MacKay family to ensure that we are always having FFEs when we are together). Five years later, we are still having fun sharing if we are having a red, yellow, or green day and why at every meal together. And, my daughter brought this tool into her workplace and uses it with her friends so they can have fun sharing their feelings and support each other. This is an example of innovation by taking a business idea and applying it to family and friends with game-changing results.

For a business example, when the tariffs crisis started, I was just thinking to myself, how are we going to 10x collaboration across the country (Canada), because that's what was going to be required to help Canadian businesses succeed. We've got over 1,200 members, twenty-six partners, over seventy chairs, and over 150 MacKay Advisors across Canada in our MacKay CEO Forums community. How do we 10x collaboration within our MacKay community so these clients can leverage their knowledge across Canada?

But it's not enough to simply have a light bulb moment and an idea. Inspired leadership translates ideas into action. Next, I reached out to a bunch of CEOs in other industries to say What do you do to bring your customers together? Is there some kind of technology that you use? How do you bring your customers together? And one of the CEOs said he had set up a WhatsApp group so all of his customers could share their knowledge and support each other. Another CEO said she was bringing her customers together to collaborate on joint events. Another CEO said he started hosting CEO dinners across Canada for his most important customers. Now, all my customers can talk about the tariffs and they can solve problems together.

I love testing new ideas such as 10x collaboration with CEOs in other industries before I take action. This approach gives me a lot of courage and confidence to either kill the idea or take action. When I come up with an idea, I'm always looking for CEOs who have been there and done that before (game changers), and then I'm more likely to be successful. And even then, if I'm not, I will simply fail fast. And that's the innovation cycle idea: find a game changer, someone who's been there and done that before, and apply your idea. If you're winning, keep going. If you're not, fail fast.

This demonstrates how continuous learning enables innovation, which enables leaders to generate new ideas and break out of the this-is-how-we-do-it trap. This mindset is fundamental to achieving innovation mastery. In my experience, individuals who are engaged in continuous learning are always in a learning environment, whether through participation in peer groups, listening to speakers, or hearing members share their challenges.

Daily Success Habits: Cultivating Innovation Daily

To consistently generate and act on new ideas, I emphasize these three success habits in innovation mastery.

HABIT #1: CREATING A NEW IDEAS JOURNAL

For me, this process often begins first thing in the morning. After a session on my Peloton, or following my twelve-minute positive intelligence practice first thing in the morning, my inspired brain is really firing, and a flood of new ideas comes to me. For some, this may happen while driving. Others may wake up in the middle of the night with a eureka moment. The crucial step then is to capture these ideas immediately in an innovation or new ideas journal, or in a monthly planning journal. This journal is not just a place to capture ideas; it's the first step in a very intentional process of innovation mastery. The ideas I capture tend to align with my ninety-day plan, which outlines my business, family, and personal goals. My brain is constantly processing these goals, so when a new idea surfaces, it's usually already aligned with my priorities for the quarter. If it's not, it might be something for a midterm or long-term plan, but it won't derail my immediate focus.

HABIT #2: SCHEDULED WHITE SPACE FOR IDEATION TIME

This might seem counterintuitive for busy CEOs who have a very full schedule. However, it's vital to block out time to access your inspired, creative brain power and think differently. I'm an early-morning person, but for others, this time might be late at night or in the afternoon; the key is to intentionally create this innovation space and block it in your calendar. It's not just about me, though. We apply this at MacKay CEO Forums with our top team. We have a top-team virtual fifteen-minute daily huddle and a "win the week" virtual thirty-minute session every week, in which we review our progress, celebrate wins, and, if we're not hitting our targets, dedicate time to coming up with new ideas and solutions. This structured approach creates continuous opportunities for innovation, moving from "win the week" to "win the month," "win the quarter," and ultimately "win the year."

HABIT 3: FIND GAME CHANGERS OUTSIDE YOUR INDUSTRY

While talking to people in your own industry can be enlightening and help you stay current with trends, it can also lead to a lack of new ideas circulating, which limits real innovation. That's why habit 3 is all about intentionally seeking out and learning from game changers *outside* your industry. The most disruptive and forward-thinking insights often come from adjacent or entirely unrelated fields. For example, innovation game changers such as Rocky Ozaki, who leads conversations on the future of work and hackathons, or award-winning CEOs who have scaled companies in completely different sectors, can introduce new ways of thinking that challenge your assumptions and expand your mental model. These are individuals who've achieved remarkable breakthroughs not by following the rules of a single industry but by rewriting them altogether. By exposing yourself to their approaches, you're more likely to spark creativity, reframe problems, and unlock solutions that would never surface in conventional circles. Make it a habit to attend cross-industry events, listen to podcasts from outside your domain, and actively build a network that includes diverse thinkers who push the boundaries of innovation.

CEO Success Story

Innovation mastery is about taking a new idea, applying it to a business function, and achieving new results. For me, it's also about fostering a continuous learning mindset and actively seeking ideas from my top team, customers, and stakeholders. I recall a compelling success story from one of the members of a CEO group that I chair.

This CEO attended a CEO peer group meeting that I was chairing, and the issue he brought to the table was that he was really frustrated with his top team because they were not hitting their targets, and he was exhausted by always holding them accountable with no new results. Month after month they were not winning, and he felt like firing all of them and building a whole new top team.

I asked, "Has anyone had a similar experience? Please share your experience of what you did to turn things around and start winning."

One of the CEOs leaned back and said, "I was in a similar situation. I hired an external entrepreneurial operating system (EOS) coach to work with our top team, and she was a game changer. She brought in all of the EOS tools, and she facilitated all of our monthly and quarterly team sessions. I learned so much about what it really takes to build a top team and problem-solve together to start winning. She also helped me face the fact that I needed to move some people off the team in order to accelerate business results. The best thing is that most of the ideas came from my top team, and because they owned the ideas, they held themselves accountable to deliver results. I'm having a lot more fun running the business, and we are all winning together."

At the end of the meeting, the frustrated CEO with the top team issue stole the idea of hiring an EOS coach instead of firing his top team. He came to the next meeting and reported that although it was a big time, money, and resource investment to hire an external EOS coach, he was already starting to see the impact of having one to help his team generate new ideas and develop problem-solving skills to accelerate business results.

Build Your Mastery: Strategies for Generating and Acting On Ideas

Ideas are powerful—but only if they are acted on. Part of building your mastery in this area includes practicing strategies for generating ideas and turning them into reality.

- **The innovation cycle—idea, game changer, action, fail fast/amplify:** Once an idea is captured, the next critical phase is finding a game changer. Sometimes, it might be someone you pay to share their expertise; other times it could be a free mentorship or even a family member. The point is, in this world of exponential change, you simply won't win if you try to do everything yourself. You must actively seek out individuals who have been there and done that before in the area you're trying to innovate in.

  Once you have the idea and you've consulted with a game changer, the third step is to apply it and take action quickly. And here's where another critical concept comes into play: fail fast, or amplify and invest more. Many leaders, because of their egos, will double down on an idea even when it's clearly not working. They'll try to force it, which results in a massive waste of time and energy. Failing fast means recognizing quickly when something isn't delivering the desired results and then pivoting without hesitation. If something's working, you keep going and amplify.

  A clear example of this fail fast principle in practice was when an alumni member of our forums approached me expressing a desire to give back and mentor our current members. I loved the idea and sought out a game changer who had successfully implemented such a program. We launched a pilot but quickly realized that finding the right match between mentors and mentees was proving far more challenging than anticipated. At that point, it was crucial to acknowledge that it wasn't working rather than push forward because I loved the idea and thought it would be a game changer for our MacKay members. That's the power of parking your ego and not being attached to the outcome (and it shows how ego mastery is so critical to innovation mastery and how interconnected all of the mastery areas are).

- **The hackathon framework:** A powerful tool we use for driving innovation, particularly from our members, forum chairs, and partners, is the hackathon framework. Our innovation game changer, Rocky Ozaki, founder and CEO of The Now of Work, brought the hackathon methodology, which originated in the tech sector, to MacKay CEO Forums. It's a structured, fast-paced process in which customers or other key stakeholders are brought together to solve a specific problem. For example, a hackathon might address the question, How can MacKay CEO Forums dramatically enhance your member experience? Participants generate ideas, build a business case, and then pitch their ideas directly to me, the CEO, all within about three hours. The beauty of it is that as the CEO, I have to commit to making a decision and taking action on one of those ideas within twenty-four hours. This process forces innovation without waiting for a crisis, such as the COVID-19 pandemic, which certainly forced everyone to innovate on the fly during a time of immense uncertainty. Hackathons create a sense of urgency and ensure that the ideas you're betting on come directly from the people whose problems you're trying to solve, leading to higher confidence in successful implementation. We successfully implemented virtual hackathons throughout COVID-19 with various stakeholder groups, including our chairs and partnership teams.

Deeper Dive: Tools and Research for Innovation

Innovation requires us to constantly challenge ourselves, to constantly grow and learn. Here are some innovation mastery tools for your leadership journey:

- **Six thinking hats:** Innovation mastery is fundamentally about taking a new idea, applying it to a business function, and achieving new results. While many approaches can foster this, one powerful tool that has truly resonated with me and my work with CEOs is Edward de Bono's Six Thinking Hats.[35]

  The Six Thinking Hats is a brilliant framework for deliberately engaging in different modes of thought during a discussion or a brainstorming session. Each "hat" represents a distinct way of thinking, allowing individuals and teams to separate emotional responses from objective facts and creative ideas from critical analysis. For instance, the Green Hat is all about creative new ideas and fostering an environment where imagination can run free without immediate judgment. This directly ties into my philosophy of creating white space and accessing one's inspired brain to generate fresh ideas, either in a team setting or while flying solo.

35 "Six Thinking Hats," De Bono Group, accessed June 1, 2025, https://www.debonogroup.com/services/core-programs/six-thinking-hats/.

Then there's the White Hat, which focuses purely on information and facts and data, ensuring that decisions are grounded in objective data. The Black Hat represents caution and identifies potential risks or reasons why an idea might not work—a necessary step, but one that must be managed so it doesn't stifle innovation. The Yellow Hat looks at the positive aspects and benefits, while the Blue Hat is the planning hat, structuring the thinking process itself.

I've found immense value in introducing this tool to top teams during my coaching sessions. It allows us to clear out the hats that often get in the way of true Green Hat thinking. Instead of getting stuck in a cycle of negativity or resistance, teams can intentionally put on their Green Hats and generate new ideas without fear of immediate criticism. This approach amplifies creativity and creates a disciplined space for innovation.

It's about understanding that every type of thinking has its place, but they shouldn't all happen at once. By consciously adopting different hats, CEOs and their teams can move beyond the this-is-how-we-do-it trap and systematically explore new possibilities. This tool, much like hackathons, transforms innovation from a spontaneous event into a structured, repeatable process, ultimately enabling leaders to generate high-impact ideas that lead to exceptional new results for their businesses and customers.

- **Design thinking:** Another powerful innovation tool is Design Thinking, particularly as applied in the book *Designing Your*

Life by Bill Burnett and Dave Evans.[36] This framework provides a method for innovating your entire life, which I find invaluable for CEOs in transition or those seeking renewed passion in their roles. It offers a robust framework to explore options, solve problems, and innovate every aspect of your life.

The method has been the subject of two PhD theses and had demonstrated significant results in helping people design the life they want. The method is centered on the principles taught in the Product Design Program and the d.school at Stanford called "design thinking."[37]

- **Fail fast methodology:** The core of this methodology, as discussed earlier, is the strategic embrace of rapid iteration: swiftly identifying when an idea is not yielding desired results and pivoting, or, conversely, accelerating investment when an idea is successful. This agile approach minimizes wasted resources and maximizes learning.

  Originating in tech, "To fail fast in Agile and Scrum is to quickly deliver increments or prototypes that can be used to validate the feasibility or desirability of a project. This approach enables rapid testing and validation of concepts and strategies to ensure that they are viable before committing extensive resources."[38] Applied in the business world, it means pivoting and moving on quickly from what doesn't work.

---

36 Bill Burnett and Dave Evans, *Designing Your Life: How to Build a Well-Lived, Joyful Life* (Alfred A. Knopf, 2016).

37 Peter High, "Two Stanford Professors Share Secrets on Designing Your Life," *Forbes*, July 10, 2017, https://www.forbes.com/sites/peterhigh/2017/07/10/two-stanford-professors-share-secrets-on-designing-your-life/.

38 Jan Neudecker, "Fail Fast," Agile Academy, accessed June 1, 2025, https://www.agile-academy.com/en/agile-dictionary/fail-fast/.

- **Relevant innovation research trends:** Staying abreast of current innovation trends is critical. For instance, the transformative impact of AI, as seen in customer service, where AI tools have replaced the need for multiple personnel and significantly boosted sales, underscores the necessity for continuous learning and adaptation.

Identify Your Game Changers: Cultivating an Innovation Network

Innovation, like all mastery areas, is deeply interconnected with relationships. It's crucial to identify game changers to develop new success habits in this area.

- **Innovation mentors:** These relationships can be formal or informal, paid or unpaid. In the context of innovation, this could involve seeking out other CEOs who are masterful at innovation and reaching out to them for feedback on their methods.
- **CEO peer support:** Beyond individual mentors, peer support is vital for innovation mastery. You can access peer support through your advisory board and board chair, who should ideally be game changers themselves. Your top team should also consist of game changers and sources of new ideas and innovation. External, cross-industry peer groups are critical for innovation mastery. Our MacKay CEO Forums, fourteen-person confidential peer support groups, focus on all aspects of diversity. Our peer groups consist of CEOs from different industries and career stages and of different genders and ethnicities, because this diversity accelerates true innovation. By

> sharing experiences in a low-ego, judgment-free environment, members gain new perspectives and steal ideas from other industries to apply in their own industry. Their peer groups give them greater courage to innovate and become industry disrupters, transformers, and leaders. Including high-impact external speakers at every meeting also fosters an environment of continuous learning and growth.

The core philosophy of You Go First inspired leadership is paramount: To inspire innovation in your organization, you must first cultivate it within yourself. This means consistently seeking new knowledge, whether through formal courses, reading, or active participation in peer groups. It involves maintaining a positive emotional state and being fully present.

END-OF-CHAPTER CHECK-IN

Rate the following on a Likert scale (e.g., 1 = strongly disagree, 5 = strongly agree), and get your score:

INNOVATION MASTERY

- I create dedicated space for reflection and idea generation in my daily routine.
- I encourage rapid experimentation and learning from failure on my teams.
- I maintain a journal or log to capture ideas as they arise.

INNOVATION MASTERY REFLECTION

Where am I playing it safe instead of experimenting? What bold idea am I avoiding because it might fail?

GAME CHANGER PROMPT

Who consistently brings new ideas to life? Who creates space for experimentation? Who could I brainstorm or cocreate with?

CHAPTER 9

ONE HUNDRED PERCENT RESPONSIBILITY MASTERY

The difficulty we have in accepting responsibility for our behavior lies in the desire to avoid the pain of the consequences of that behavior.

—M. SCOTT PECK

Every day, during our fifteen-minute top team huddle, we celebrate the wins of each person on our top team and we ask for help. We do this to build our individual and team mental fitness and to get greater access to our positive brains to reduce stress, improve relationships, and maximize performance. I typically go last on the daily huddle unless there is something really critical that needs to take up our daily huddle time. We believe that every win is a team win and every issue is a team issue (breaking down silos happens on a daily basis through our daily huddles). At the same time, we want to build our individual mental fitness on a daily basis so we can each take 100 percent responsibility for our individual and team results and behaviors.

I've learned that it's much easier to take 100 percent responsibility if I have strong mental fitness and I'm accessing my positive brain instead of my fear brain. I've always been at the bottom of our organization chart because I see my CEO role as helping everyone on my top team win. When my top team is winning, it is focused on helping our customers and our entire MacKay CEO Forums community win. I have a mindset of taking 100 percent responsibility for all results and behaviors for the entire company—the buck stops with me! It's a very empowering way to live my life and avoid showing up in ego talk—playing the blame game, getting defensive, being right, looking good, and criticizing others. Taking 100 percent responsibility is the opposite of ego talk.

I've come to understand that truly inspired CEOs—those who earn lasting respect and drive extraordinary results—publicly give credit to others for all successes and never seek public praise when things go right. Instead, they take 100 percent responsibility for privately patting themselves on the back to celebrate personal wins, build their self-confidence, and maximize their performance. They don't need external recognition because they have their own, personal recognition based on how they define success in their CEO role. I challenge CEOs that I coach to use a 5:1 ratio of positivity to negativity on a daily basis, for themselves and for their top teams. If you catch yourself and your top team members doing things right using a 5:1 positivity ratio on a daily basis, then you and your entire team will be in a much better position to take 100 percent responsibility, stepping up and shouldering the full weight of responsibility when things go wrong. You and your top team won't deflect, make excuses, or throw others under the bus. You'll understand, deep in your core, that taking 100 percent responsibility creates a culture of learning and growth and treating everything that happens as a gift.

It's about stepping back from any high-stakes situation and asking, *every single* time something doesn't go the way you hoped, "What can I do to accept this situation?" "How can I treat this as a gift and learn from it?" "What part did I play in this?" or "What could I have done differently? And what action can I take to move things forward in a positive direction?" This 100 percent responsibility approach is much more effective when compared to a victim consciousness approach of "I can't believe this happened," "This is really bad," "Whom should I blame," "They should never let this happen," or "I'm going to tell them that they screwed up, and they are making me look bad."

Consider the case of Howard Schultz. In 2008, after stepping back into the CEO role during a period of declining performance, Schultz took full responsibility for Starbucks's problems, including overexpansion and a decline in customer experience. Rather than blaming the economy or external factors, he acknowledged that the company had lost its way. [39]

When you stop assigning blame—whether to colleagues, clients, family members, or external conditions—and start looking inward for growth and treating everything that happens as a gift, you reclaim your power. It's not about self-criticism or blaming others; it's about becoming a lifelong learner. In doing so, you not only become an inspired leader but a more grounded, intentional, and better version of yourself every day. Taking 100 percent responsibility transforms you from a victim of circumstances into a powerful agent of change. It's an incredibly empowering way to navigate life, freeing you from

---

39 Greg Petro, "Starbucks Has Lost Its Way (Again), and Founder Howard Schultz Knows Why," Forbes, August 16, 2024, https://www.forbes.com/sites/gregpetro/2024/08/16/starbucks-has-lost-its-way-again-and-founder-howard-schultz-knows-why/.

the helplessness and frustration that often come with feeling like things are out of your control. For me, this is the core of inspired leadership—taking 100 percent responsibility with zero excuses.

Daily Success Habits

To cultivate a mindset of 100 percent responsibility, I coach CEOs on several daily habits that reinforce this leadership approach.

HABIT #1: BUILD ON STRENGTHS

This habit is about intentionally focusing your time and energy on your areas of greatest strength. StrengthsFinder 2.0 by Gallup is a CEO tool I've mentioned that I've been using for the past twenty years to help CEOs identify and build on their strengths. It's also a great team-building tool for top teams to identify and build on their strengths. When you operate from your strengths, you save a lot of time, you become more resourceful, you make better decisions, and you are more effective at problem-solving. As a CEO, your role involves privately recognizing and celebrating your strengths and publicly recognizing the strengths of others, making it a point to catch yourself and everybody else doing things right on a daily basis using a 5:1 ratio of positivity to negativity and giving them full credit for their wins. This way when you need to have difficult conversations with your top team about their results and/or behaviors, they know that you have their backs and want to get them set up for success. This isn't just about external validation for your team. It builds their mental fitness, self-confidence, and self-esteem. Catching your team doing what's right goes beyond morale boosting to reinforcing those strengths you want your team to continue to develop.

HABIT #2: MENTAL FITNESS MANTRA

The highest-impact 100 percent responsibility CEO coaching tool that I also use personally is a mental fitness mantra.

I use a very simple and powerful daily mantra to help me take 100 percent responsibility for my behaviors and results. It consists of four simple statements that I repeat several times a day to interrupt my ego/judge and get me into a positive emotional state, especially when I get bad news or when I'm preparing for a difficult conversation:

"I'm enough. I'm a gem. I'm a beautiful person. I'm a lovable person."

This mantra reminds me that no matter what happens I can show up as the best version of myself every day and take 100 percent responsibility.

It helps me prepare for difficult conversations and helps me recover from them.

This daily mantra allows you to face challenges head-on, knowing you have the capacity to influence outcomes, rather than succumbing to external pressures or criticisms.

HABIT #3: FIFTEEN-MINUTE DAILY TOP TEAM HUDDLES

At MacKay CEO Forums, we use a structured approach to foster a culture of 100 percent accountability. A practical way to implement this is through daily fifteen-minute huddles with your top team. During these virtual team huddles (we are a fully virtual national team), each person quickly shares the following:

- a win for the day, to build their mental fitness
- what they plan to accomplish that day, to hold themselves accountable, as we believe in self-accountability

- what help they need from the team, to build team accountability to support each other

This simple, consistent practice ensures everyone is aligned, quickly identifies potential roadblocks, and reinforces a shared commitment to outcomes. This structured approach extends to weekly, monthly, quarterly, and annual check-ins, creating a continuous feedback loop that fosters a culture of 100 percent accountability.

CEO Success Story

I've seen firsthand how profound the shift to 100 percent responsibility can be, and also the serious consequences when CEOs refuse to make this shift.

One particularly poignant story involves a CEO I coached who was constantly in conflict with his board chair. The board chair, who was the former CEO of the company, frequently micromanaged him. The CEO felt constantly undermined, believing he could never be good enough in the eyes of his predecessor. Their relationship was a perpetual head-butting match. I repeatedly tried to coach him on the principle of 100 percent responsibility. I emphasized that he needed to focus on his own actions and how *he* was showing up, regardless of his board chair's behavior. This meant learning to park his ego and put his judge in the box so that he could show up as an inspired CEO.

Despite my coaching, he was unwilling to truly commit to this 100 percent accountability approach. He couldn't let go of blaming his board chair, convinced that the problem lay entirely with the other person. He remained fixated on how his board chair *should* behave, rather than how *he himself* could respond. He started talking to other board members about his frustrations with the board chair. Ultimately, this approach led to his being fired. This was a painful yet transformative moment for him. We then had to work on accepting this new reality, which is a significant part of taking 100 percent responsibility. He had been giving away too much power by constantly obsessing over the board chair's supposed wrongdoing rather than empowering himself to act differently. Over the next ninety days, we embarked on a deep dive, working through a plan that helped him understand what truly got in the way of him showing up as his best self, independent of external circumstances. He learned to own the outcome and ask, "Is there something I can be doing differently?" instead of feeling like a victim. This was a profound shift from playing the blame game to showing up as an inspired CEO and taking 100 percent responsibility for his results and behaviors.

Another CEO faced a different kind of crisis: He lost his biggest customer. His initial reaction was to blame everyone else. He felt he had been working 24/7 and simply didn't have the support he needed. He wallowed in a "woe is me" mentality. I challenged him to accept the reality of the situation and then, crucially, to take 100 percent responsibility for the loss and to treat it as a gift and a profound learning and growth opportunity for his entire team. This was a difficult pill to swallow at first. However, as he leaned into it, he realized that accepting responsibility actually felt empowering. It freed him from feeling like a helpless victim of circumstance. He found relief from the stress, frustration, and sleepless nights that had been causing him a lot of suffering. We established that taking 100 percent responsibility doesn't mean you have to do *all* the work yourself. It means you own the ultimate outcome and strategically figure out who needs to be in place to ensure you achieve your ideal results. It means treating everything that happens as a gift and opportunity for learning and growth for you and your team. It means having the courage to step in and step up when necessary, rather than waiting for others or for external conditions to change.

These stories highlight a critical point: Your ego often gets in the way of taking 100 percent responsibility. It wants to make others wrong, to find fault outside yourself, and to keep you stuck in a cycle of blame. Overcoming this judge—the part of your ego that whispers criticisms and excuses—is absolutely essential for truly mastering 100 percent responsibility.

Build Your Mastery

Achieving 100 percent responsibility mastery requires specific tools and a consistent commitment to changing ingrained patterns.

- **Embracing a zero excuses mindset:** This is about making a conscious and unwavering choice to take full responsibility for every outcome in your life. It's the antithesis of the victim mentality. When something goes wrong, instead of immediately looking outward for blame, you turn inward and assess your own role, even if it's just your response to the situation. You treat everything that happens in life as a gift and opportunity for learning and growth. This mindset is incredibly empowering because it puts you in control rather than leaving you at the mercy of circumstances or other people's actions.
- **Building a self-accountability culture:** When you make a commitment to be on time for meetings or deliver results on your ninety-day plan, you hold yourself accountable for your behaviors and results. You share your ninety-day plan with your top team, and you invite all top team members to share their ninety-day plans with the top team to build a

self-accountability culture. If you often blame your team for missed deadlines or not meeting targets, self-accountability would challenge you to own the outcome. This might mean re-evaluating your delegation strategy, providing clearer expectations, or offering better support. The goal is to consciously choose to own the outcome and then determine what you can do differently to achieve a positive result. If you model self-accountability with your top team, every person on your top team will want to follow your lead.

- **Apologizing effectively:** Apologizing effectively is a powerful tool in taking 100 percent responsibility. It's often incredibly difficult because the ego resists it, preferring to make others wrong. But the ability to genuinely apologize shows that you are a lifelong learner and that you believe that feedback is a gift to help you learn from your mistakes and move on.

  The methodology involves the following steps:

  - **Step 1: Become aware:** Recognize when you've made a mistake, contributed to a conflict, or failed to deliver results. Say to yourself, "I choose to accept that I made a mistake."
  - **Step 2: Take ownership:** Critically assess your contribution to the problem. This isn't about accepting all the blame but about genuinely owning your part in a failed relationship, a lost customer, or any other disruption. Ask yourself, "Is there something I could have done differently to prevent this situation?" and "What did I learn from this situation?"

- **Step 3: Apologize sincerely:** Deliver your apology, whether it's one-on-one, to your board, or to your top team. This act, free of excuses, is incredibly powerful.

  "I would like to apologize for any upset that I caused during our meeting," or "I would like to apologize for not delivering the results for this quarter," or "I would like to apologize for not communicating my expectations effectively," and "I would like to share what I've learned from this difficult situation and what I plan to do to ensure it doesn't happen again."

  When facing a potentially difficult conversation after an apology, tools such as MVE (mirror, validate, empathize) can be invaluable. This framework allows you to show up as a CVA (caring, vulnerable, and assertive) human being, acknowledging the other person's perspective without getting pulled into their negativity, even if they continue to express anger or frustration.

Deeper Dive

The journey to 100 percent responsibility mastery requires understanding yourself and leveraging key insights from thought leaders.

- **The role of vulnerability:** For me, vulnerability is about learning to park your ego and show up as your real, authentic self. Your ego, that inner judge, constantly tempts you to criticize yourself, others, and your circumstances. It thrives on playing the blame game, making you defensive, and pushing you to always look good, never lose face, and be right. To truly take 100 percent responsibility, you must learn to quiet this inner judge and operate from your positive, inspired brain for most of your waking hours—aiming for 80 percent is a great goal. This vulnerability means openly admitting when you've made a mistake or contributed to a negative outcome, whether it's neglecting your health or failing to invest in a key relationship. It's a brave act that disarms conflict and builds trust. I've mentioned the impact Eckhart Tolle's book *A New Earth*, in particular chapter 3, had on me, marking the beginning of my deep understanding of how ego can impede success—and how it is the opposite of vulnerability.

- **John Izzo's *Stepping Up*:** A significant thought leader for me in this area is John Izzo, who wrote the book *Stepping Up*. This book articulates what it means to step up and take 100 percent responsibility, not just for yourself but for your team and everyone around you. It delves into the specifics of how this mindset liberates you from feeling like a victim and empowers you to proactively shape outcomes. It provides a detailed road map for embracing this level of ownership in all areas of your life. Chapter 5 focuses on the 100/0 Principle (100 percent responsibility and zero excuses). It means zero excuses for not taking the action you are able to take, regardless of what others are doing or not doing.[40]
- This book articulates what it means to step up and take 100 percent responsibility, not just for yourself but for your team and everyone around you. It delves into the specifics of how this mindset liberates you from feeling like a victim and empowers you to proactively shape outcomes. It provides a

40 John B. Izzo, *Stepping Up: How Taking Responsibility Changes Everything*, 2nd ed. (BerrettKoehler Publishers, 2020).

detailed road map for embracing this level of ownership in all areas of your life. Chapter 5 focuses on the 100/0 Principle (100 percent responsibility and zero excuses). It means zero excuses for not taking the action you are able to take, regardless of what others are doing or not doing.

Identify Your Game Changers

You don't have to achieve 100 percent responsibility mastery alone. Here are some of the game changers I appreciate:

- **Board chairs and trusted sounding boards:** My own board chair and mentors are people I can reach out to when I feel overwhelmed or frustrated or fall into victim consciousness. Through our conversations, they help me return to a mindset of 100 percent responsibility and accountability. My husband and business partner is masterful at challenging me to take 100 percent responsibility in all aspects of our life—business, family, and personal. I've hired numerous external coaches over the past twenty years who have helped me learn how to show up as the best version of myself. This underscores the importance of having individuals you trust who can help you refocus and take ownership.
- **Medical doctors/health professionals:** Over the past twenty years, I've witnessed far too many CEOs ignore bad health news or even avoid getting important tests because avoidance seems easier. But 100 percent responsibility for your own health matters more than anything else in life. Deep down, we all know when we're not eating right, not sleeping enough, indulging in bad habits, or not exercising. It's too easy to fall

back on excuses (especially, as we discussed in other chapters, the I-don't-have-time trap). But excuses are simply that: an avoidance of 100 percent responsibility. Medical doctors, personal trainers, nutritionists, health coaches, and other health professionals are vital because they provide guidance and support, helping CEOs shift from an excuses mindset to one of full ownership and proactive health mastery.

END-OF-CHAPTER CHECK-IN

Rate the following on a Likert scale (e.g., 1 = strongly disagree, 5 = strongly agree), and get your score:

ONE HUNDRED PERCENT RESPONSIBILITY MASTERY

- I take full ownership of my actions and their outcomes, even when it's hard.
- I regularly privately acknowledge my successes and failures without seeking external validation or recognition.
- I resist the urge to blame or make excuses, focusing instead on learning and growth.

ONE HUNDRED PERCENT RESPONSIBILITY MASTERY REFLECTION

Where in my life am I still holding on to blame or excuses? What would full ownership look like in that situation?

GAME CHANGER PROMPT

Who holds themselves accountable no matter what? Who could support me in stepping up and taking full responsibility?

CHAPTER 10

SHARED EXPERIENCE MASTERY

Successful people become great leaders when they learn to shift the focus from themselves to others.
—MARSHALL GOLDSMITH

Shared experience mastery is a fundamental component of inspired leadership and is defined as the ability of CEOs to inspire others to take positive action by authentically and nonjudgmentally sharing their experiences, real stories of the mistakes they've made and lessons they've learned, rather than simply telling others what to do. This approach is crucial for mentoring and developing future leaders through impactful storytelling and knowledge sharing.

The Core Philosophy: Inspiring Action Without Telling People What to Do

The essence of shared experience mastery lies in its departure from traditional top-down leadership styles (some might use the term *command and control*). Instead of dictating actions, inspired leaders empower others by sharing their own journeys, including both successes and mistakes, in a way that resonates and motivates. This approach fosters a judgment-free environment in which individuals feel safe to learn and grow.

I've learned that telling people what to do rarely works—it often leads to defensiveness or inaction and may come across as condescending. Instead, people are far more likely—in my experience, nine times out of ten more likely—to take action when they feel empowered to solve their own problems. That's why I lean into coaching questions and powerful, real-life stories filled with mistakes and lessons learned. I've moved away from the outdated mindset that CEOs need to have all the answers or boss people around. In my world, *boss* isn't a badge of honor—it's a term we've left behind. Today's leadership means you go first—inspire yourself and then inspire others by sharing your experiences when your top team members come to you with problems. They will then follow your lead and share their experiences with their top teams, and this approach will speed up results throughout the entire organization.

Daily Success Habits

To truly master shared experience, you need to cultivate specific daily habits that foster genuine connection and understanding.

HABIT #1: PRACTICING 80 PERCENT LISTENING/20 PERCENT TALKING

This is a critical daily success habit, and frankly, it's one that most CEOs really struggle with. They're used to being the smartest person in the room, the one with all the answers. But when you are truly listening, you can influence far more effectively. It enables you to hear others' perspectives with genuine curiosity and without judgment. You are not listening to solve the other person's problem. You are listening to think about a story you can tell that might help the other person solve their own problem. This active listening is the essential first step before you can effectively choose whether to share experiences, use coaching questions, or give advice. Let's face it, we all know how to give advice and tell people what to do. A more inspiring approach, in most cases, is to either use storytelling or coaching questions to help other people solve their own problems, giving advice as a last resort.

Often, when a CEO comes to me with a problem, say with their business partner, and they recount the conflict, I ask them about their own behavior in the interaction. Nine times out of ten, they admit they were doing all the talking. This isn't about blaming; it's about recognizing that active listening skills are paramount. When you listen to the other person, you gain a lot more ability to influence. Why? Listening 80 percent gives you the opportunity to get curious and really understand the other person's perspective, and acknowledge their perspective without judgment, before responding with your own point of view and/or shared experiences.

HABIT #2: BUILDING YOUR FLUENCY IN LANGUAGE THAT FOSTERS CONNECTION AND BUILDS TRUST

This habit goes hand in hand with listening. It involves developing fluency in powerful communication tools we've discussed, such as CVA and the MVE tool kit. MVE, in particular, forces active listening because you must literally repeat back or mirror what the other person said.

HABIT #3: IDENTIFYING SHAREABLE EXPERIENCES

This is where the art of storytelling comes in. Most CEOs I work with, despite having a wealth of experiences, don't naturally possess the skill set for impactful storytelling. It requires conscious practice and, often, the guidance of professional coaches. I've personally invested hundreds of thousands of dollars in speaking coaches to continuously improve my storytelling. Writing books, such as this one, also forces me to take my storytelling to the next level.

Your stories need to be compelling, succinct, and high impact. They also benefit from having a bit of drama and from your being vulnerable by sharing the mistakes you've made, which makes CEOs human and more approachable. When the outcome wasn't a foregone conclusion, it shows a journey, making the story more relatable and powerful. Crucially, these shared experiences must be relevant to the discussion at hand. Every time I think about a story, I'm thinking about an example of how I solved a problem that might be helpful for the person who has a similar problem to solve. Stories without a direct relevant solution to a problem can waste a lot of time.

CEO Success Story

I often see variations of this play out with the CEOs I coach. For instance, I recall a CEO who was incredibly frustrated after a meeting with her CFO. She came to our session visibly angry. I guided her through a series of questions: "Did you engage in active listening?" "Did you prepare your response using the MVE tool kit?" and "Did you share any relevant experiences or ask coaching questions?" Her answer to all of these was no. She admitted that when she gets emotional, all those tools simply go out the window (which is why emotional mastery and ego mastery are so important).

This is a common CEO challenge, but it's also where the power of shared experience truly matters. In our confidential peer groups, when a CEO shares a struggle like this, other members who have been there, done that will often share their own true stories and experiences. Sometimes, these stories are about having literally been fired or pushed out for showing up in an ego-driven way with a board member, biggest customer, or business partner. These powerful, authentic stories influence CEOs to reflect deeply. They leave the meeting, often going back to apologize to key stakeholders, saying, "Hey, my ego got in the way. How do we get this back on track?" These are incredibly happy stories for me, as I see people realizing the power of this approach and that it's possible to repair the damage of important relationships before it's too late.

I think of the times, during the five-minute sharing sessions, when a CEO has said they were certain they were going to be fired by the board (or actually *were* fired by their board). The stories of other CEOs, their experiences, how they handled it, their mistakes—and then how they turned it around—are probably the most impactful shared experiences.

I also have inspiring stories in which a CEO, after being coached using shared experience, successfully rebuilt trust in a difficult relationship simply by apologizing and showing up as a CVA human being. And of the CEO who felt miserable after selling his business and, through ISAR coaching (discussed in a moment), shared his own happy story about starting all over again. These examples demonstrate that shared experience is not just about avoiding failure; it's about showing up as the best version of ourselves (most of the time) and building future leaders who can learn from our successes and from the mistakes that we've made.

Build Your Mastery

To effectively leverage shared experience, I rely on a structured approach that makes storytelling impactful and efficient. Over the past twenty years, CEOs have been using our shared experiences approach to leadership (ISAR framework) during all confidential peer group meetings. We don't allow advice giving, and that's exactly why we are able to support CEOs on their inspired leadership journeys. We challenge all of our members to bring these skills to their top teams to build future leaders, speed up succession planning, and accelerate business results.

THE ISAR FRAMEWORK (ISSUE, SITUATION, ACTION, RESULT)

This framework is an easy and effective way to relate successes and failures and expedite problem-solving. It's a structured approach that ensures stories are clear, concise, and impactful.

Here's an example of a shared experience using the ISAR framework:

Joe's CEO challenge: "I think I need to fire my CFO because he doesn't get along with other members of my top team. I've been telling him to stop getting into conflicts with his peers, but he's not listening."

A CEO peer shared experience using the ISAR framework:

- **Issue:** "I was in a similar situation with my CFO, and I was about to fire him because I was getting too many complaints about him from my top team. I got along with him really well, but he kept getting into conflicts with his peers."

- **Situation:** "I'm not a CPA, and the thought of firing my CFO was causing me a great deal of stress. I thought maybe I could hire a CFO coach to help him with his people skills."
- **Action:** "I reached out to my CEO coach to see if she could recommend a CFO coach. Fortunately, my CFO accepted the invitation to work with a highly recommended CFO coach, and the 360-degree coaching program was a game changer for him."
- **Result:** "The CFO apologized to his peers for his behaviors and asked them to give him ninety days to prove that he would make changes to his leadership style. He asked them for support by sharing feedback with his CFO coach, and he gave a weekly update on his progress. I was so relieved that I didn't have to fire my CFO and inspired by his commitment to learn new leadership skills."

Joe listened to the above story and was inspired to get introduced to the highly recommended CFO coach as a potential solution to his challenge. He also asked to get introduced to the CEO coach so he could be an exemplar for his CFO before recommending that he work with a coach.

If the CEO peer had used an advice-giving approach like Joe—"Don't fire the CFO; you should hire a coach like I did"—it's unlikely that Joe would have been inspired to take action, not only for his CFO but for himself. This ISAR framework ensures that stories of successes and mistakes become powerful lessons learned, transferable to others in order to inspire positive action.

The Benefits of a Two-Minute Leadership Storytelling Format

In today's AI-enabled, exponentially changing world, time is of the essence. We are bombarded 24/7 with everything from texts to global news to relentless business demands. My goal is to make every interaction highly impactful without wasting precious time. That is why I advocate for a two-minute leadership storytelling format.

At MacKay CEO Forums, we live this principle: We have fifteen-minute phone calls, meetings, and daily huddles. Each CEO in our peer groups gets only five minutes to deliver all their business, family, and personal updates and present an issue or opportunity they need help with (and we hold them to it!). When we share experiences, each person has just *two minutes* to tell their story. We even use a timer in our meetings so we can start on time and end early! This forces conciseness and enables active listening. This very fast-paced, time-effective way of developing CEOs accelerates performance, and we challenge our members to use the same approach with their own top teams.

EXPERIENCE-SHARING TECHNIQUES THAT EMPOWER OTHERS

The ISAR model itself is a powerful experience-sharing technique. The goal is to get people to think in terms of stories, to literally rewire their brains to look for opportunities to share valuable insights. This is a new leadership tool kit for most CEOs who join our peer groups, which is why many struggle when they are put on a podium or a panel. They need to learn how to tell compelling stories that are succinct and high impact to inspire people.

When you master this leadership approach, you can inspire yourself daily by reflecting on the learnings from your mistakes and successes and treat everything that happens in life as a gift. And you can feel good about sharing what you've learned to build future leaders at work and with your family. It forces you to reflect on your purpose and passion. This, in turn, empowers others. By sharing your journey—your mistakes, your lessons learned, your positive successes—you make it much more likely that others will courageously take action and do the hard work needed for their own growth and development.

Deeper Dive

At the foundation of this practical application, there's a science to effective storytelling and mentorship.

BUSINESS STORYTELLING EFFECTIVENESS

Consider this: As of this writing, there have been nearly a quarter of a million TEDx talks.[41] Stories resonate. But researchers such as Paul Zak have shown that the release of brain chemicals such as oxytocin during storytelling helps create trust.[42] Another group of researchers used actual brain scans to demonstrate how the brain changes as stories are told.[43] It creates a kind of brain "coupling," in which we feel we are sharing in the experience as well.

41 TEDx Talks, YouTube, accessed July 1, 2025, https://www.youtube.com/user/TEDxTalks.

42 Paul J. Zak, "The Neurobiology of Trust," *Scientific American* 298, no. 6 (2008): 88–92, 95, https://www.jstor.org/stable/26000645.

43 Uri Hasson et al., "Brain-to-Brain Coupling: A Mechanism for Creating and Sharing a Social World," *Trends in Cognitive Sciences* 16, no. 2 (2012): 114–121, https://doi.org/10.1016/j.tics.2011.12.007.

BEST PRACTICES FOR EFFECTIVE MENTORING

Effective mentorship, in my view, is not about telling someone what to do, unless they have absolutely no experience or frame of reference. For instance, a newly appointed CEO presenting to their board for the first time has no experience, so direct advice might be the best approach to start with, followed by sharing experiences and asking coaching questions.

However, in most situations, the best approach is likely a combination of sharing experiences and coaching questions.

- **Coaching questions:** These are my go-to questions:
    - What's your ideal outcome?
    - What do you need to do to actually achieve that ideal outcome?
    - What are you prepared to commit to as a next step?

These types of coaching questions help individuals solve their own problems, fostering self-reliance and increasing their likelihood of taking positive action. Combining coaching questions with sharing experiences is a very effective approach to mentoring and building future leaders.

Identify Your Game Changers

When I reflect on the biggest breakthroughs in my life—personally and professionally—they've all come from reaching out to the right people (game changers) rather than trying to figure everything out on my own. Early on, I realized that success doesn't come from isolation but from finding people who have been there and done that before and have achieved the goals that I've set for myself. I learned that asking for help from people who would be willing to share their experiences would not only save me a lot of time but would give me greater courage and confidence to achieve big goals. And I learned that leading with generosity and sharing my experiences with others (being a game changer for others) would enable me to make the biggest contribution to the people around me. I made a conscious decision to surround myself with game changers and to be a game changer for others.

One of the very first career game changers in my life was instrumental in helping me get my PhD done part-time in three years while I taught full-time at Lincoln University in New Zealand. I moved to New Zealand from Canada in 1991 because I accepted a three-year job at Lincoln University as a lecturer. One of the conditions of the job offer was that I needed to enroll in their PhD program. It was a very exciting career adventure, but I had no idea how I was going to get a PhD done in three years part-time (in a new country where I didn't know anyone).

I remember thinking two things: *Who on the planet has already achieved this goal (of doing a PhD in my area of research interest)?* and *Who might be willing to share their experience with me?* I also thought, *How might I lead with generosity and offer to help them first?* I did some searching on the internet, and I reached out to the leading professor in my field, who was based in Philadelphia. He shared with me that he had always wanted to do a sabbatical in New Zealand. I shared with him that I wanted him to help me get my PhD done part-time in three years. We became game changers for each other, helped each other achieve our goals, and became lifelong friends (until he passed away from pancreatic cancer at a very early age). I'm so grateful for all of the game changers in my life who have inspired me on my journey, and I take the time to express my gratitude at every opportunity.

The two powerful questions above have saved me years of effort and have assisted me in identifying game changers who have helped me achieve all of my business, family, and personal goals. I've had the honor and privilege of being a game changer for others by leading with generosity and sharing my experiences. Game changers have also helped me avoid the classic lonely-at-the-top trap.

I'll be the first to admit that when I launched MacKay CEO Forums, I did not know how to scale a business. But I didn't let that stop me, and I sought help and guidance from various game changers. One of the first things I did was share my vision with the CEO peer group I was chairing at the time. I was transparent with them—I told them I planned to grow the organization significantly and that I would need their help to do it. During that phase, I made it a point to listen to them differently. I tapped into their collective wisdom, truly valuing their feedback, insights, and lived experiences. Their perspectives were incredibly helpful and challenged me to think bigger and more strategically.

In addition to my peer group, I formed an advisory board made up of game changers (incredibly successful business leaders), many of whom were already members of MacKay CEO Forums and had scaled much larger companies than mine. I handpicked people I admired and respected, and their guidance became instrumental in helping me navigate the complex journey of growing the business. They helped me see around corners, avoid common pitfalls, and make smart decisions I might have missed on my own.

One of the most pivotal relationships in my journey was with Bob McDonald, a highly accomplished CEO. Very early on, I approached him and asked if he'd consider being a mentor to me. Even though I was just getting started, I led with generosity—I offered to help him however I could. To my delight, he said yes. What followed was the beginning of a true mutual mentorship and friendship. His mentorship helped shape my vision of what MacKay CEO Forums could become—a network of connected, high-performing peer groups across the country. He joined the CEO peer group that I was chairing at the time, and I became his CEO coach. I look back on that decision to reach out to him as one of the smartest and most rewarding decisions I ever made. He's a game changer in my life, and we've been close family friends for over twenty years. I hope that I've been a game changer for him too!

This idea—of seeking out game changers for every major goal—has become a core principle in my life. Whether the goal is in business, family, or personal growth, I always start by asking two powerful questions: Who has been there and done that before and can help me do this smarter, faster, and with greater courage and confidence? And, How might I lead with generosity to help them? That one daily success habit has had a compounding effect on every success I've achieved.

And that's exactly the culture we've built at MacKay CEO Forums. It's a very inspiring community of successful Canadian business leaders, designed to be an ongoing source of game changers who share experiences and connect. Our confidential peer groups bring together fourteen high-performing CEOs who are all committed to learning, growing, and supporting one another. There are no competitors in the room, and it's a safe, judgment-free zone where people talk openly about everything—business, family, and personal things. We believe in parking our egos, telling the truth, sharing lessons learned, and showing up for each other during the inevitable bumps in business and in life. That culture, built on mutual respect and shared stories, consistently sparks breakthroughs and accelerates performance.

END-OF-CHAPTER CHECK-IN

Rate the following on a Likert scale (e.g., 1 = strongly disagree, 5 = strongly agree), and get your score:

SHARED EXPERIENCE MASTERY

- I avoid telling people what to do and instead use coaching questions and shared experiences to inspire others.
- I lead with generosity and I'm a game changer for others, sharing my mistakes and lessons learned to help them achieve their goals.
- I look for game changers to help me achieve all of my business, family, and personal goals so I can learn from their mistakes and successes (which is a lot more fun than learning from my own mistakes).

SHARED EXPERIENCE MASTERY REFLECTION

What's a personal story I haven't shared yet that could inspire or support someone else on their journey?

GAME CHANGER PROMPT

Who has helped me feel safe enough to share my story? Who models authentic, judgment-free storytelling? Whom can I practice with?

CHAPTER 11

SOCIAL CONTRIBUTION MASTERY

Success cannot be measured in wealth, fame, or power, but by whether you have made a positive difference for others.
—RICHARD BRANSON

I can remember how excited I was when I realized that growing MacKay CEO Forums into a multi-million-dollar company could take the impact of what we were doing way beyond the initial ten peer groups of CEOs I was chairing and coaching and create a more exponential contribution. If we could have ten thousand CEOs in our peer groups, then their influence on their people and beyond would have a positive impact on millions of people around the world.

For far too long, the traditional view of leadership has focused solely on the bottom line. But as I've learned through my decades of experience working with thousands of CEOs, true inspired leadership extends far beyond mere profit. It's about recognizing the profound impact your business can have on the world, and more importantly, the impact it can have on *you*. Once you commit to showing up as the best version of yourself every day (i.e., an inspired leader), so that you can make the biggest contribution to the people around you, your CEO role becomes passion, fulfilment, and pure joy. This is the essence of social contribution mastery.

Defining Success: Business as a Force for Good

At its core, social contribution mastery is about intentionally leveraging your passion, your strengths, and your purpose to make a meaningful difference in the lives of others. For me and for MacKay CEO Forums, our dream is to populate the world with inspiring leaders. This isn't just a company purpose; it's my personal purpose, and it guides every decision I make, whether it's related to our business, my family, or my personal life. When you embrace the social contribution mindset, your business truly becomes a force for good.

Success in social contribution means asking yourself, "What is the difference I want to make in other people's lives?" and "Why does this really matter to me personally?" These questions become a powerful filter for every yes and no you utter, whether it's about volunteering your time, making donations, or even structuring your business model. With so many demands on CEOs' time, you must be very intentional with your choices.

One of the most concrete ways we see this commitment manifest in the business world today is through the B Corp movement. About ten thousand companies globally across 160 industries, employing more than a million people, currently hold a B Corp certification.[44] The movement is growing, and it's a powerful testament to CEOs' willingness to take a stand on business as a force for good. It's a rigorous strategic planning certification, demanding a significant time commitment, but it encourages businesses to think beyond just profit, considering people and the planet in equal measure.

For us at MacKay CEO Forums, in 2018, pursuing B Corp certification was a no-brainer. It wasn't just about getting a certificate; it became a strategic planning tool, a standard of excellence that pushed us to consider how we could make the biggest possible contribution. It serves as a road map for continuous improvement in areas such as diversity, inclusion, sustainability, and employee well-being. By becoming B Corp-certified, we became an exemplar for others within our community, inspiring our members, partners, and chairs to consider this path for their own organizations.

However, social contribution isn't solely about formal certifications. It's about a fundamental shift in mindset. Many CEOs and business leaders mistakenly believe that their ability to contribute to society is reserved for retirement, or that it's an obligation rather than an opportunity for personal fulfillment. This couldn't be further from the truth. The world expects CEOs to step up and contribute while we are in the game of business, because that's when we have the most influence to inspire others and get them involved in important causes. When you align your personal purpose and passion with your company's mission, your volunteer time no longer feels like a sacrifice but rather an extension of what you love to do. This alignment is a

---

44 B Lab Global, "Over 1 Million People Now Work at Certified B Corps, as New Global Research Highlights Leadership on Fair Work," press release, July 28, 2025, https://www.bcorporation.net/en-us/news/press/over-1-million-people-now-work-at-certified-b-corps/.

huge part of maintaining your passion and feeling a profound sense of purpose every single day.

Daily Success Habits: Leading with Generosity

One of the most impactful daily habits for fostering social contribution is adopting a mindset of leading with generosity. This is a fundamental pillar of our MacKay culture and a core tenet of the You Go First philosophy.

What does this look like in practice? It means that every interaction you have, whether with a customer, a supplier, a business partner, a peer, a team member, or anyone else, should begin with the question "How can I help you?" Most people operate with a transactional mindset, thinking, *What can this person do for me?* But when you lead with generosity, you flip that script. Your primary focus is on helping them be successful.

Only once you have genuinely helped that person be successful, then, and only then, can you ask, "Well, how can you help me?" You don't keep score. Instead, understand that by contributing to the success of others, you build a powerful network of goodwill and positive energy that will ultimately come back to you, often in unexpected ways. It's not a one-to-one exchange but a ripple effect. We've seen this firsthand at MacKay CEO Forums, where we've helped over five thousand Canadian business leaders over the past twenty years by consistently leading with generosity. We invite people to our events, encourage participation, and constantly look for ways to help them get connected to game changers who can help them achieve greater success in all areas of their lives.

This mindset is also crucial for CEOs when they are approached for various commitments, such as cutting a check for a charity, sitting on a board, or volunteering their time. Since you can't say yes to everyone, having a clear purpose and passion serves as your filter. For example, ask yourself, "What breaks my heart?" Then say yes to opportunities in business and in the nonprofit sector that will fill your heart with joy. If the opportunity aligns with your purpose—for example, my purpose of populating the world with inspiring leaders—then it becomes a meaningful social contribution that fuels your passion.

From a business standpoint, I love CEOs, and what breaks my heart is that it's so lonely at the top. My dream is that every single CEO on the planet learns how to become an inspired leader, so it doesn't have to be lonely at the top. CEOs sacrifice their physical and mental health, their marriages, and their important family relationships because they think that's the only way they can be successful CEOs. Most CEOs aren't even aware that peer support exists to help them achieve success in all areas of their lives. This lack of awareness is such a huge loss of CEO potential!

From a volunteer standpoint, over the past five years, I've been on the advisory board of the GenWell project, a registered charity that is all about Canada's human connection movement. It's not just lonely at the top; social isolation after the pandemic hit an all-time record around the world. It's an honor and a privilege to be on the board of an organization that has been recognized by the World Health Organization for its work on social health. And Canada's human connection movement is totally aligned with my purpose, filling my heart with joy.

When you engage in volunteer work that is truly aligned with your purpose, it doesn't feel like a burden or a *should*; it becomes another source of energy and passion. CEOs, with so many demands on their time and treasure, have to find that symbiotic relationship between giving and personal fulfillment.

CEO Success Stories

I have countless stories of CEOs who have embraced social contribution in remarkable ways, transforming their businesses and their lives in the process.

One powerful example comes from Rick Hansen, famous for his Man in Motion World Tour. While Rick operates in the nonprofit sector, his story profoundly impacted my own journey toward embracing social contribution. I was captivated by the immense difference he made in the world, dedicated to finding a cure for spinal cord injury and creating accessible buildings for people with disabilities. He completed a legendary twenty-six-month, thirty-four-country, forty-thousand-kilometer wheelchair journey around the world. His goal was to create a more inclusive world in which barriers are removed and people of all abilities have the opportunity to reach their full potential.

Meeting Rick was a game-changing moment for me around social contribution; he showed me what was possible when someone truly leveraged their strengths, skills, and passion for a cause. His dedication prompted me to ask myself, "What am I going to do, using my strengths and passion, to make a difference?"

The goal is to be just as passionate about the causes you support as you are about the business you're running.

Build Your Mastery: Aligning Purpose and Engaging Teams

To truly master social contribution, you need strategies that align your efforts with your core purpose and effectively engage your team.

Engaging other executives and employees in social contribution is also vital. This includes encouraging your top team to participate in social impact initiatives. It can be as simple as incorporating social contribution activities into team building. Many of our CEOs' top teams already contribute to various charities, whether in music, the arts, or sports. The challenge is to encourage them to act collectively, fostering a shared sense of purpose and contribution. Employees are increasingly seeking employers who actively care about their community and provide opportunities for them to contribute, such as days off for volunteer work. They want their jobs to align with their values.[45] This is how you embed social contribution within your company.

When you lead with social purpose, you become an exemplar. You are able to inspire your employees to step up and make a difference. This means thinking about how you are treating your people, considering aspects such as parental leave, time off, and supporting volunteer work. The B Corp certification, for example, looks at all these metrics, including diversity across all stakeholders: your board, top team, customers, suppliers, and business partners. It's a comprehensive approach to ensuring your business practices reflect your commitment to social impact.

It's important to remember that leaders often face the challenge of saying yes to too many things, leading to burnout. Social contribu-

45 Philip Mirvis, "Engaging Employees Who Care About the World: From What I Need to Who I Am," *Organizational Dynamics* 52, no. 2 (2023), https://doi.org/10.1016/j.orgdyn.2023.100979.

tion, while rewarding, must be balanced within your one hundred waking hours and your time-mastery plan. There are different phases of life in which you might need to adjust your level of involvement. For instance, when my kids were young, I stepped off all volunteer boards because I needed to prioritize my family and business, choosing instead to contribute financially or recommend others. The key is to set boundaries so that you don't resent the commitments you've made to make a difference.

Identify Your Game Changers: Community and Contribution Partners

Just as in other areas of mastery, identifying your game changers is crucial for advancing your social contribution.

In the realm of social contribution, your game changers might include the following:

- **Social impact mentors:** These are individuals who have successfully integrated social purpose into their lives and businesses. They can offer guidance on navigating the challenges and opportunities of leading with a mission. Rick Hansen is certainly a game changer for me in this regard.
- **Community leaders:** Look around your community. Local leaders, whether in nonprofits, government, or other sectors, often have a deep understanding of those community needs and existing initiatives. They can help you identify where your contributions can have the most impact.
- **Contribution partners:** These could be other CEOs, organizations, or individuals who are already making significant

social contributions. Collaborating with them can amplify your efforts and provide shared learning opportunities. For example, my eight-year volunteer involvement with Canada's Great Kitchen Party, a social enterprise that aims to celebrate and connect the diversity of Canada, has allowed me to inspire many within our MacKay community to volunteer together, amplifying our collective contribution. It auctions off exciting trips and has raised millions for youth initiatives. Not only is it fun—it's fun with a cause.

The goal is to surround yourself with game changers who inspire you to make a greater contribution, aligned with your passion, to help others be successful. Leverage the wisdom of others who have successfully navigated the complexities of social impact so you don't have to figure it all out alone.

END-OF-CHAPTER CHECK-IN

Rate the following on a Likert scale (e.g., 1 = strongly disagree, 5 = strongly agree), and get your score:

SOCIAL CONTRIBUTION MASTERY

- I consciously lead with generosity in my professional and personal interactions.
- I actively contribute time, money, and/or expertise to causes aligned with my values.

- I evaluate new opportunities based on purpose alignment and emotional resonance.

SOCIAL CONTRIBUTION MASTERY REFLECTION

When was the last time I asked "How can I serve?" What might shift if I led with that question more often?

GAME CHANGER PROMPT

Who is a role model for giving back? Who's deeply aligned with their purpose and community impact? Who could help me find the right cause or opportunity?

ACKNOWLEDGMENTS

I would like to thank the more than five thousand Canadian CEOs, executives, and business owners who, over the past twenty years, have joined a MacKay CEO Forums peer group and are on the journey of learning how to inspire themselves and their top teams. Thank you for giving credit to your peers, your forum chair, and the game changers in your life. They have helped you achieve extraordinary success in all areas of your life. Thank you for inspiring me to continue to populate the world with inspiring leaders.

ABOUT THE AUTHOR

Nancy MacKay is the founder and CEO of MacKay CEO Forums. Nancy founded the company in 2005 because she could see that it was lonely at the top. That's exactly why the company has offered confidential peer support to over five thousand Canadian CEOs, executives, and business owners. Nancy is the best-selling coauthor of *I Don't Have Time!* and she enjoys playing squash and doing Zumba.

LET'S CONNECT

Thank you for joining us on this journey toward inspired leadership and mastery.

If this book resonates with you or sparks ideas for yourself, your team, or your organization, we'd love to hear from you. At MacKay CEO Forums, we work with purpose-driven CEOs, executives, business owners, and forum chairs who are committed to accelerating growth, saving time, and making a bigger impact.

Please reach out, whether you're interested in

- hosting a keynote on inspired leadership, time mastery, or building high-performance cultures;
- joining a confidential peer learning group;
- exploring partnership opportunities; or simply
- continuing the conversation.

Our team is here to support you. You can learn more at www.mackayceoforums.com or reach out directly to our team at **inquiries@mackayceoforums.com**.

Follow and connect with us on LinkedIn:
https://www.linkedin.com/company/mackay-ceo-forums/

We look forward to being part of your leadership journey.

Together, we can build a more inspiring world, one leader at a time.